Transforming The Co-dependent Woman

Sandy Bierig, M.Ed., C.A.C.

Health Communications, Inc.
Deerfield Beach, Florida

Sandy Bierig
Spirithaven
1600 Falmouth Rd., Suite 175
Centerville, MA 02632

Library of Congress Cataloging-in-Publication Data

Bierig, Sandy
    Transforming the co-dependent woman/by Sandy Bierig.
    p. cm.
    ISBN 1-55874-115-1
    1. Co-dependence (Psychology) — Popular works. 2. Women
 — Substance use. 3. Women — Psychology. I. Title
RC569.5.C63B54   1991
616.86'0082 — dc20   90-4919
                                     CIP

© 1991 Sandy Bierig
ISBN 1-55874-115-1

Publisher: Health Communications, Inc.
            3201 S.W. 15th Street
            Deerfield Beach, Florida 33442-8190

Dedication

To my children, Brian, Kurt, Terrie and Bob. Had I been smart enough to know it when we were all younger, I would have told you that we do not waste them if we grow through our pain and tears. How well we live after that depends on our generosity of spirit and our willingness to love freely, no matter what might tempt us to do otherwise. It is nice to know that you didn't need me to tell you all that.

Acknowledgments

I want to thank my partner, Ruth Fishel, for the support which led me to write this book. I have serious doubts that I ever could have finished it without her faith in me and her encouragement. While I have come to expect them from her, I hope I never take them for granted.

Bless Marie Stilkind, my editor, whose patience and kindness have graced my struggle to write the truth as I have seen it.

My colleagues and friends in the field of recovery, especially Judith DeStefano, Maureen Lydon, Eileen White and Cathy Blum who work tirelessly for the good of women, refusing to allow them to be hurt anymore if they can possibly help it.

Contents

Preface

The day is not far off when women will stop being obedient to the old images of themselves as somehow less than males. This is an especially important change in attitude. Whole lives have been wasted while women waited for, rather than demanded, the ordinary respect that they give men, and that men give to each other.

Our daughters and their daughters after them must rise up and insist on their rightful place in the emerging society of the '90s. They cannot afford to give in to the pressures which come from every side to be passive and to wait for their needs to be met. They must come to understand that meeting those needs is synonymous with creating and maintaining a healthy community. They must be equal partners with men in that creative effort. They cannot afford to sit back and trust that everything will work out in the end.

When we are sick spiritually, we must take an active role in healing ourselves. No one else can make the decision to do it for us, and no one else can really know what we need unless we tell them. Therefore, to the extent that we decide to stop living in silence with our fear and guilt and shame, just to that extent will we make progress along the road to recovery.

But I couldn't count the number of times that women who are new to recovery have told me that they like men more than women, that they are much more comfortable with men than with women. Such attitudes point right to

the crux of the problem: which is that women are socialized to think of themselves as inferior to men, as less
interesting, as less trustworthy and certainly as less able
to offer the support and guidance that men are capable
of giving.

At no time in this book do I intend to denigrate men in
general. On the contrary, women have a great deal to
learn from them about how to set goals and how to feel
worthy as human beings. Perhaps there should be a college course that only women may attend. It could be titled
MEN, 101, and it could be taught by members of that
small but wonderful group of men who consider themselves feminists. The whole purpose of the course would
be to destroy stereotypes about both men and women,
and to spur some real thinking and attitude-changing on
the part of the students.

No one should read this book without keeping in mind
the *how* of recovery, that is, honesty with self, open-
mindedness about all current beliefs and willingness to
change attitudes when they are barriers to lasting recovery.

Finally, all of the examples in this book really happened,
but those involved have been disguised. To all of you, I say
thank you and wish you the comfort of knowing you will
never walk this road alone again.

With love and faith,
Sandy Bierig

Introduction

If I am I because I am I,
And you are you because you are you,
Then we both exist;
But, if I am I because you are you,
And you are you because I am I,
Then neither of us exists.

— *Rabbi Mendel*

With this one sentence, Rabbi Mendel has explained with eloquence and simplicity just what *co-dependence* is and what it is not. There are as many faces of co-dependence in women as there are women suffering from it. At bottom, it is a soul-sickness that is likely to be found in anyone, anywhere. It can't be cured by pills or by magic, but recovery is possible.

Women who function *independently* find their own purpose and reasons for existence. They then build on them, finding fulfillment and rapport with others throughout their lives, finding interdependence with others.

Interdependence means I can lean on you and you can lean on me when either of us is facing more than we can handle alone. It means that you are my friend and I can trust you to be there when I need you if you possibly can. Just as importantly, it means you can also trust me to be there for you. It does *not* mean that we do for each other what we can do by ourselves. It does not mean that we write each other's life scripts or that we seek to be dependent on each other.

We have the luxury of letting go of each other so that we may each lead our separate lives, experiencing ourselves in any way we find fulfilling. It means that I can respect your choices and your right to make them, even if I am worried about how they will turn out for you. And it means that I can rejoice when you are happy and cry with you when you are sad, without needing to take credit for or change the way you feel.

In an interdependent relationship we are free to be ourselves, to allow ourselves to change, to encourage growth in ourselves and each other. We can learn from our mistakes, rather than seeing them as proof of our inadequacy because we cannot tolerate imperfection in ourselves.

Women who are co-dependent may also be alcohol- or drug-addicted. They may have an eating disorder or some other dysfunction. They come from all walks of life. They are found among the rich and the poor, the privileged and the deprived. They are members of minorities. They are young, old, attractive or not. No one type of person is invulnerable to the pain of co-dependence.

If the goal for these women is to achieve interdependence with others, then still more people will be affected in some way when they do. If we think of the problem in this light, then we can see the issue has enormous implications.

If we think of their recovery as the act of claiming their own power, then we see that someone is going to lose it. It's an exciting prospect to think about being involved in the process in a very fundamental way. While fear of the unknown is certainly present, the prospect of people all over the world liberating themselves from self-imposed prisons more than outweighs any prospective negative outcome.

CHAPTER 1

Co-dependence And Women

Women caught up in co-dependence can do none of the things their interdependent sisters can do. There is too much at stake for them to let go of anything or anyone they think they need. They have too much to lose to risk changes in the status quo and cannot afford the kind of generosity of spirit that allows interdependence with others.

When we take a look at co-dependence we see certain sets of behaviors which clearly define persons who cannot stand alone and who have great difficulty pairing with others. Women who are co-dependent have certain circumstances which complicate their lives and their recoveries enormously.

In the extreme, co-dependent women need to control everything as well as everyone around them. Only in this way can they make themselves feel they are all right, that they are valuable, that they matter.

1

They live alone with their shame and fear, torturing themselves regularly with accusations that they are not good enough. They feel insecure, as if they are getting by on fakery. They believe if anyone really knew them, they wouldn't be accepted because they would be despised. Women can go on for many years this way, believing they are fooling everyone.

It's important not to be fooled by surface appearances in co-dependent women. Just as there are many co-dependent women, there are degrees of being stuck in the self-defeating behavior they exhibit. Because they believe they are inadequate and fear being found out, some co-dependent women will try to make themselves indispensable to the people in their lives. Married women staying at home caring for their children and their husbands are particularly well-suited to this tactic. On the surface these women seem to have it all together, functioning independently — until we come to understand their motives for the things they do. Some never come to realize what valuable human beings they are to be able to maintain such incredible effort.

Still other women cling to the people around them, fearing to live life on life's terms, never risking to grow as individuals. (Certain service jobs lend themselves well to this behavior.) As a result, they never find the security that comes with learning to trust themselves. And they never seem to realize that the people in their lives who allow this clinging are just as needy.

The following example demonstrates just how all-encompassing such effort can be.

Lois:

My husband wanted to come home and read his paper and eat his dinner quietly without having to listen to the chatter of our children as he ate. So, wanting to keep him happy and allow the kids some fun at the table, I served him in the living room on a TV table while the children and I ate in the dining room.

I did a lot of things like that, always trying to keep my husband happy, while carrying the bulk of the parenting responsibilities. It made me feel important and useful. It never occurred to me that I was a lot more like a doting mother than a wife or partner to my husband.

Since I started recovery and began to understand my co-dependency, I can't believe I went that far trying to please him. Whenever he criticized our children, I took it personally, feeling he was finding fault with me. It never occurred to me that he was being selfish and self-centered or that he was not sharing in the upbringing of our children. I did not see myself as being fearful and dependent.

Looking back, I realize my behavior was learned watching my mother and father interact. She was very subservient to him and he took full advantage of it. I must admit I took everything a lot farther than my mother ever dreamed of doing.

I grew up being very afraid of my father and of men in general, for that matter. The man I married was my father all over again, except that he was not physically abusive to me.

Lois' co-dependence kept her looking in the wrong direction for her sense of self-worth. She paired inevitably with a man who was simply not interested in any but his own wishes and needs, and his needs could only be met by someone like Lois. As his perfect mate, she allowed her own needs and wishes to be stifled in favor of meeting his and by doing so settled for less every day of their lives together. He, on the other hand, was incapable of making any real connection with his wife on a feeling level. He really did not like women much. He felt threatened by them so he kept them at arm's length.

Recovery for Lois meant being open to learning about her own needs and making changes in herself that would allow for self-honesty. After that she had to be willing to grow emotionally and spiritually, no matter how much pain she had to go through.

Lois also had to be willing to risk her marriage because her husband was not happy to see the changes in her. He was threatened by them. He wanted her to remain the same so he could stay in charge of the relationship.

He knew when Lois was really determined about something, she dedicated herself to it completely. He was sure this time would be no different. All of the other times, though, she had eventually tired of chasing results that had never materialized and reverted to being docile and attentive to him. He was worried this time, however. Somehow this seemed different.

Lois' husband was correct in his instinctive assessment of her dedication to her recovery. Her life was finally making sense to her. She was no longer depressed and hopeless and saw real possibilities in her future. Her self-esteem was receiving a real boost in the process of her recovery and she began to understand that she'd been settling for less all her life.

She hoped her husband would come to understand the transformation she was undergoing and appreciate and value it as much as she did. Lois wanted him to join her in working out the differences between them that were becoming more apparent each day.

He could not, however, find it in himself to appreciate anything she did if it didn't benefit him directly. He neither appreciated nor valued her achievements because they didn't center on him. On the contrary, they were very threatening for exactly that reason.

Fortunately for Lois, she did not give up hope that she would one day find the quality that would make the difference in how she felt about herself. She was so sure when it came along, it would improve her life.

Co-dependence Or Dependence?

Co-dependence is often confused for simple dependent behavior on people, places or things. Actively drinking alcoholics, for instance, exhibit dependent behavior on alcohol. Their whole lives are arranged around ensuring the continued flow of the alcohol. Nothing is too great an obstacle if overcoming it will ensure their supply. But alcohol does not need anyone. It's not capable of thought or feeling or wanting. It's an inanimate object, a thing.

The people who manufacture spirits are another story. They know from their research that 70 percent of all alcohol is bought by alcohol-dependent people, which includes more and more women all the time. The manufacturer's very livelihood is dependent on maintaining and increasing sales. The alcohol industry as a whole, therefore, is dependent on alcoholics. The circle is complete. The alcoholic is a co-dependent with the alcohol producers and they with the alcoholic. Both need each other in a very fundamental way.

Co-dependence requires human interaction and the need for each other at a basic level of existence. The definitive word here, then, is **need.**

Whenever a woman believes she can't manage, can't be happy, can't even survive without having a particular person in her life, she can be described as being dependent on that person.

When that person in turn feels compelled to depend on her to the same degree, these two people can appropriately be described as being co-dependent. What they perceive to be their need for each other will doom them to a prison of their own making. Anything new or out of the ordinary is a threat to their co-dependence. The very *idea* of change can't be tolerated. Only their *need* for each other can be served fully.

We see this effect frequently among older married couples. She has spent her life at home, taking care of her husband and children. She has not learned to drive, handle her own money or made any major decisions affecting her own life. Retirement may mean she is whisked away from the grandchildren she dotes upon to a community where her husband can play golf or fish 364 days a year (he does not play on Christmas). When, as is usually the case, he dies before she does and leaves her a widow, she is lost and alone in a world she had no conscious part in making.

What happens to a woman like this depends on how lucky she is in having people around her who will pull her along toward independence. If her own will to survive is strong enough, she'll join them in the effort. If it is not, she'll probably continue to stay home, acting as if nothing has changed in a practical sense. She may, as some research indicates, start drinking as a way to cope with the loneliness. Or she may look for other people, like her children, on whom to depend, thinking she cannot stand on her own two feet.

What Do We Mean By Need?

Men and women have a basic need to pair off, to be members of a community and to be important to certain others in their lives. Recovery programs call them "instincts for sex, society and security." Since they are basic drives, they impel human beings to satisfy them. These truly are needs in every healthy, natural and normal sense of the word.

However, although this might not be a very popular notion, I don't believe people *need* to have certain individuals in their lives. Rather, although the word *need* is used a great deal, healthy people make choices about whom they *want* to have in their lives. People make free and satisfying decisions about just who fills their romantic dreams, who will be the best life partner and whose ideals are closest to their own. But they don't try to bind those persons to them hand and foot, trying to control their every move, assuring the perfect outcome for every action.

A *healthy* pairing of individuals is based upon mutual decisions made for the purpose of sharing one's life with an individual who can add quality to life. In the process, the basic needs for "sex, society and security" are met and exceeded by having one's wants met as well.

The Co-dependent Mold

In order to understand how co-dependence happens, picture an actual mold created for use early in a child's life. This mold should be fitted with hooks which can catch and hold two people in a more or less rigid position. The hooks are made of things like opportunity, financial or other forms of insecurity, repetition, fear and the possibility of loss, of being alone, the fear of abandonment, the fear of not being loved at all or of having love withheld.

In the dysfunctional early home of the co-dependent woman, she begins life in this mold, very much under the control of one important person, usually a parent or parent figure.

While children are wonderful observers, they don't have the knowledge or experience to interpret what they see. That's why the people around them become so important when they interpret how the child should think, feel and act. Consistently and pervasively, the child is molded by this person. The less healthy the influence, the less healthy is the child and the family system.

Healthy home or not, there is no more powerful influence on the growth and development of a child than the parent figure. Children brought up by active alcoholics, untreated adult children of alcoholics, child abusers, etc., are seriously affected for life by the influence exerted by these people, unless appropriate treatment is received. Behavior patterns formed by such children as coping mechanisms become deeply entrenched at a subconscious as well as a conscious level. This means any changes must be made later internally as well as externally.

Because one cannot give away what one does not have, co-dependent parents pass on co-dependent behavior. So a daughter might learn at Daddy's knee that her job in life is to be pretty, accommodating and a source of pride to him. If she fails at these tasks, the result is disapproval or punishment. Frequently she infers from this punishment that she deserves to feel ashamed of herself.

The father in this case might be a person who defines himself by the way the elements of his life appear to be, even though in reality they are very different. Therefore, his family must always appear wholesome, close-knit and happy or his sense of self is damaged. These two people end up being caught in the grip of yet a third entity: the image.

There is no self-deceit that is impossible for a person dedicated to preserving an image if that person has based his or her life entirely upon it.

For this father, the death of the image is the same as the death of self.

Eventually, the children of such a narcissistic man hardly seem to exist as separate entities. Unable to break the control this primary relationship has on their lives, they become convinced they must need this control. They believe that without it they are inadequate. For them, everyone they meet becomes an opportunity to get life right, to receive love, to be fulfilled and to value themselves.

Apropos of this kind of co-dependent bonding, I am reminded of the woman who was telling her friend about her plan to visit her mother to make amends for her abusive behavior (while living in her mother's house) during her drinking years.

This trip, she told her friend, was the third such visit. On the other two occasions her mother had treated her and her apologies with disdain and had made it clear she would not forgive her daughter for her behavior. After hearing this story the friend said, "Let me get this straight. It sounds as if you are going to continue to make amends until your mother gets it right."

In fact, both mother and daughter had a perfect co-dependent relationship. The daughter's feelings about herself were still being filtered through years of looking to her mother for answers as to what these feelings should be. The mother purposely kept her daughter dependent upon her. She was always there with money or offers to take care of her children. At the same time, she tied her daughter to her by withholding approval of anything the daughter did that could help her cut her apron strings.

One of the interesting things about such relationships is that the participants in them believe that they are acting out of love for each other . . . which is why it takes so long for them to see what they are. Every "I love you" is just another link in the chain binding them together. In fact, love has nothing to do with it. Each person acts out of what she perceives to be necessary to meet her own needs.

To demonstrate the impossibility of living life fully — or even in the present — while being trapped in a relationship based on this kind of need, pick up a folding chair or some other kind of light chair and hook it over your arm. Now picture yourself going through one ordinary day in this manner. It wouldn't be long before you said to yourself that you couldn't do it — and you would be correct!

Until such women as the mother and daughter in the preceding example are able to grasp that they are indeed co-dependents and that they are living in the past, they remain in denial, unable to change their patterns.

The daughter in this example could never have learned to trust herself while growing up. By insisting on having the last word on anything her daughter did, the mother gave a clear message to her daughter that she was not able to make her own decisions. The mother was petrified to be out of control. If we run back to the generation before the mother, we would probably see a domineering parent there, too, who was also a controlling, invalidating person and so on, back through time.

Such relationships do not occur in a vacuum. That is why it is so important to break the cycle of co-dependence. Otherwise it will just go on and on, ruining and wasting lives, generation after generation.

Co-dependent Values Stand Until Challenged

By their nature, children are very much the center of their own universe. Because they occupy such a prominent place in that world, parents exert a tremendous influence over the shape their children's thoughts and opinions take. If they've been born into co-dependent family systems, children will only know how to function accordingly. Because they've been built from the earliest years, value systems formed in the formative years stand until challenged.

Yet challenge of this sort is a highly threatening, incredibly difficult thing for co-dependents to do. They already lack the self-esteem which would bolster them. They also fear the loss of the people around them who might misunderstand or blame them for embracing those new values.

When a family unit has been built upon co-dependence disguised as loving interaction, it's like a fly being caught in a spider web. The more the fly struggles, the more it's caught by the sticky strands. Finally, it becomes enmeshed in the web, at which time the spider can gobble it up.

Co-dependent relationships are like a spider web to the people caught in them. The sticky strands represent rules governing every behavior. There are no loopholes and punishment is doled out for any transgression — real or imagined. Anyone trying to break out of the web is a huge threat as well as a potential rebuke to its very fabric.

When the threat is perceived, therefore, all members of the relationship automatically respond to the danger. They must be ever more vigilant and more creative in their efforts to maintain the status quo. Much of this iron-framed structure is created at such a subconscious level, it takes a long time to perceive it at all.

Since co-dependent relationships are formed from the inside out, that's also the only way they can be changed and only by each participant individually. Such change is only possible after co-dependent patterns are recognized and rationalizations protecting them are successfully challenged.

It's this last aspect that contains the potential for the greatest harm and paradoxically, the most hope for freedom in the future. The decision to live one's life for someone else is the very heart of co-dependency. Recognition of that choice is the first, best hope for change.

It's an amazing thing to watch a thought-controlled person wake up to the reality of that control. She comes wide-eyed and joyful, surprised, sad and frightened to death at the implications. Many women describe this time as one in which they felt a great burden had been lifted and they felt a great sense of freedom. They begin to feel really clean for the first time, while anger and then sorrow are released.

People are creatures of habit and they are driven by instincts for self-preservation which demand a sense of security about where they fit among their contemporaries. I think the vast majority of them must feel safe in their surroundings and that they are important to at least one other person. Such powerful needs can and do create whole societies dedicated only to their own continuation.

Examples of co-dependent relationships on a huge scale are legion throughout history. George Orwell wrote about just such a society in his fictional *1984*. In it, everyone had to conform or the whole social structure would come crashing down. For their own survival, their governors had to be completely vigilant to ensure that no one wavered in his or her conformity. In too many instances, we've seen totalitarian governments operate much like this.

In the early days of this country, slaves depended entirely on the plantation owners for food, clothing, shelter and for decisions about what would happen to family members. In order to keep them controlled, slaves were not allowed to move about the country freely or learn to read and write. The purpose for all this, of course, was to create prosperity for the plantation owners. Both groups needed each other to maintain this way of life. In this case, it took a presidential proclamation and the willingness of a lot of good people on both sides to force change.

During World War II, the German people had a co-dependent relationship with Adolf Hitler. They made him their leader to improve their standard of living. Without their total commitment to him, Hitler would not have

been able to wreak the havoc he did. Together they
formed the fiction of Germans as Master Race. As Hitler
fell from the weight of his own lies, the Master Race
foundered and fiction ended. Unfortunately, the cost in
human and material terms was enormous.

CHAPTER 2

Socialized
Co-dependence

In this country, women are socialized to be subordinate at every level to the male and to his institutions. Even in this relatively enlightened time, women still earn only $.65 for every dollar the average male is paid. In the home, most women are still charged with the full responsibility for its upkeep, as well as the care and feeding of the children. It doesn't matter whether or not the women work outside the home.

Wives are still considered responsible for providing sexual release for their male partners. Although not exclusively, as research has repeatedly demonstrated since the first appearance of the Kinsey Report.

I saw a talk show on television once during which the panelists, all male, were admitting openly that they had sex with women other than their wives. A guest psychologist said it's a common occurrence. Whereupon the host-

ess asked for a show of hands from women in the audience who were still married and believed their husbands
had been unfaithful during their marriages. Predictably,
not one hand went up.

One can guess what was going on in the minds of that
audience to keep them from admitting the truth. Certainly
there was fear of admitting such a thing openly; fear of
what others would think of them; fear their husbands
would find out. All that fear of being shamed, of losing
security, of failure, was probably wrapped up in a great
big bundle of denial that their husbands could ever do
that to them.

These are the same kinds of fears that burden co-dependent women from their earliest years. Fear itself is a
tangible commodity to them. It can become a sickness in
itself, preventing them from changing by not allowing in
new information.

It is the same thing that is at the bottom of sexism,
bigotry, racism and prejudice. This kind of fear is of loss
of self, of the sense of who one is, and of the loss of self-
esteem. It involves all kinds of value judgments and demands a great deal of control over one's environment. It
works strongly against intimacy with people because it
brooks no disagreement or interference of any kind. The
attitude toward the world must be, "I must be right. Therefore it follows you must be wrong." There can be no
middle ground and no compromise.

Fear of this sort creates fertile ground for the pall of
denial to set in, enveloping reason and stifling hope. Wom-
en affected by it are perfect pawns for those willing to
use their fear for their own ends. Its power was well
understood by the opponents of the Equal Rights Amend-
ment, for instance. Proponents explained innumerable
times that it represented a simple matter of taking women
out of their second-class citizen status. However, the wom-
en opposing it would not accept responsibility for their
own lives for fear of losing control over the few advan-
tages they perceived to be theirs at the time, such as
financial security. It was a self-defeating bargain for hu-

mankind, and one which will go on constricting our daughters, and sons, for years to come.

To recover from co-dependency is to be willing to challenge everything one has heard, has read or been taught because so much of it is simply not true. Three examples come to mind of unreasonable, emotional outcomes which occurred as the result of rigid socialization:

The Co-directors

The first involves two women who co-founded a human service agency. Next, they put together a good working Board of Directors who were responsible for policy decisions. Last, these women, with the approval of the Board, agreed to work side by side as co-directors of the agency, sharing the work load and receiving equal salaries.

After operating smoothly in this manner for several years, someone on the Board decided that the two women needed to change their titles and their salaries, to put one of them in charge of the other and to be paid more. The Board member saw this as a move to bring the agency into line with others in the state which operated that way. If most agencies ran that way, the member felt, it was probably a good way.

He did not, however, take into account the needs and wants of the two women. They felt they were performing equally and could tolerate the relatively low salaries they received because they knew the money came from the donations of people who, like themselves, really cared about the work they were doing.

Eventually, because they were strong women who were sure of themselves and the way they wished to work, the issue was dropped. They went on working with the same titles as before and with equal salaries. In this example, the Board Member was fearful that since the agency was not doing everything the way others did, there must necessarily be something wrong with their organization.

The Foundation Application

The second example involves the agency I co-founded, which operated on behalf of women recovering from alcoholism and drug addiction. Here, the same kind of fear-based prejudice came into play when our agency applied to a foundation for supplemental funds for the operating program.

At the preproposal conference, the applicant agencies were told that first-time applicants were almost never successful in achieving grants. Indeed, when the review of our proposal came back, it showed that we had been refused. The reasons given were that (1) more documentation was needed and (2) that the balance of the Board of Directors, most of whom were women, needed to be changed from more to less than a majority of recovering alcoholics.

If there was any perception on the part of the foundation of just how insulting this second demand was, there was no indication of it. To our credit, the agency decided to withdraw its application permanently and seek funding elsewhere.

The Work-Training Project

The third example took place several years ago when we had a lot of ideas and no money at all. My agency, Serenity, Inc., applied to a government organization to fund a work-training project we wanted to start.

To our great pleasure, our proposal was approved for a $50,000 grant and we were given a list of stipulations in writing and one only verbally. We could easily have lived with the written requirements, but the verbal one was absolutely out of the question. That one called for us to have a male in charge of the project or, regardless of the legality of this, we would not receive the funding.

There was no possible way that we would be coerced into submitting to this requirement, but it was not because we did not want to work with men. Even if we had a man in mind at the time, we would have still found this requirement absolutely insulting and arrogant to the women on our Board and in our management. To have accepted it would have been to fail as role models to the women in our program who had come to us with the intention of moving past the artificial barriers in their lives.

By far the majority of volunteers in this country are women, but most of the CEOs of the large agencies are men. That is not so amazing as is the fact that women tolerate such a state of affairs. Once again, I believe it's due to the fear women have of changing their place in society in any but a relatively superficial way. It's a refusal to broaden their comfort zones by taking appropriate risks.

Old Ideas Die Hard

College women still suffer greatly from this fear of success as has been shown over and over again in polls taken to profile young people. Normal anxiety about outcomes is misread by both the women experiencing it as well as the others in their lives as a lack of self-confidence and is therefore a precursor to failure.

When Representative Geraldine Ferraro of New York ran for vice president and later Representative Patricia Schroeder of Colorado considered running for president, we still heard the ridiculous talk about women being unable to hold high office because of their supposed instability "at that time of the month." This in spite of such outstanding leaders in both the past and in the present as Golda Meir of Israel, Indira Gandhi of India, Margaret Thatcher of the United Kingdom, Benazir Bhutto of Pakistan and Corazon Aquino of the Philippines.

Women are judged by different standards than are men because they are judged on the basis of how they've been socialized. This automatically devalues them when they are compared against the achievements of men. Women hadn't even been allowed to vote in this country until relatively recently. They were not sent to schools of higher education, were shut out of technical fields or were trained to do the more menial tasks in such fields. One of the funnier lies is that women are too delicate: they faint at the sight of blood. Yet who was it throughout history who nursed the injured and the sick, often without any help or advice?

Women are stuck in a kind of apartheid here. There are only a few states, Alaska, Wyoming and North Dakota in which there are currently more males than females in the population. It seems that now more than ever, men and insecure women are afraid of losing their control over the way society is constructed. This is, of course, one of the major concerns in the abortion issue. If women are allowed to control their own bodies, the possibilities for change in the fabric of society are enormous. What will happen to the "Father knows best" axiom? Who will take care of the women who have been convinced that they are not capable of taking care of themselves without the help of some man?

I believe these attitudes will go the way of the woolly mammoth. They will be relegated to the form of extinction reserved for things that no longer serve any kind of useful purpose. The result will be more freedom and partnership for all people in their relationships and more real opportunities for their children to explore themselves much more fully as functioning human beings.

CHAPTER 3

Co-dependent Women And Addiction

Another pattern of co-dependency is the addiction to alcohol and drugs of many adult daughters. Having been raised in the same dysfunctional, alcoholic home as her nonaddicted siblings, she suffers from the identical learned behavior patterns. The difference is that she adds dependence on a chemical to her repertoire of dysfunctional behaviors. It's interesting that many of the same co-dependent behaviors the addict learned while growing up are called upon in the growth of her disease.

Co-dependent alcoholics seek constant affirmation and approval from those still around after the drinking has stopped. This is the same behavior which led to the bottle in the past. The sad truth is that no one can ever receive enough approval from others if self-approval and self-affirmation are not present. This is the motivation that is behind the behavior of the active alcoholic who continually moves from person to person, group to group and bar to bar looking for people who will offer approval and a sense of belonging.

Co-dependent alcoholics must receive approval and affirmation from some other source if they are to approve of themselves. But they can't receive it from parents who never learned to develop it and therefore couldn't pass it on to their children. They can't receive it from people who see their behavior as self-destructive and they can't receive it from people who will not be pulled into the uncompromisingly bleak world of co-dependence and/or alcoholism or drug addiction.

The Nature Of Addiction

Before I talk about addiction in depth, it would be a good idea to explore the nature of addiction itself. First, I think for addiction to be present we must be affected in all of three ways: physically, mentally or emotionally, and spiritually. If we are not affected in all three ways, then I believe that whatever we are experiencing is something other than addiction and needs to be handled differently.

Second, under the control of addiction, all people lose their ability to act in their own best interests. That's why alcoholics can literally drink themselves out of marriages, relationships, jobs and into death. This desperate attribute of addiction is hardest for those around alcoholics to understand because they measure it by rational standards of behavior.

An addict believes she *must* have her drug of choice. She needs it to feel normal. She does not recognize that "normal" is relative, that "normal" varies at different times in anyone's life.

An example is a woman who believes she can't dance in public unless she's had a few drinks. When she realizes that it was her body, her feet, her sense of timing and rhythm that allowed her to dance when drinking, that the drug had only relaxed her inhibitions, she is amazed to recognize she can indeed dance. In this case, education has brought a change of understanding and understanding, in turn, expands the ability to experience life in yet another way. As this person undergoes a metamorphosis in her knowledge of herself, normalcy occupies an expanded space.

I believe addiction is forever. It's possible to stop doing or using what one is addicted to, but it's not possible to do it or use it just a little or once in a while. It's also not possible to use substitutes that produce the same kinds of feelings as the original addiction while waiting for a cure.

Methadone, for instance, was supposed to help heroin addicts wean themselves off heroin. What it actually does is create a bridge from heroin to more easily obtained drugs like alcohol that they may never have used otherwise. Also methadone is a less destructive drug in the sense of how much damage its users do to society, but I have been told by many addicts that it's harder to withdraw from than heroin.

Clients in one drug program I know of used to work to earn drinking privileges toward the end of their treatment. But instead of being able to handle alcohol like social drinkers, the clients found themselves having added alcohol addiction to their problems, for which they then needed more treatment.

The heart of the program I co-founded in 1974 was a recovery home for women who came from a wide variety of backgrounds and whose ages ranged from 18 to 70. Their alcoholism had reduced them to a point where they needed almost total care to achieve recovery and independence. Becoming alcohol- and drug-free was only the start of their recovery. In order to stay that way, they needed to come to grips with their own dependencies.

At the time we opened the program, the dependence of addicts on substances (and on people) was not as well understood as it is now. There was only a small amount of written information on women who were addicts and there were only 30 other programs for women throughout the country. Much of our treatment, although based on some very firm principles, was formed through trial and error.

We believed our program should be open to all women regardless of race, creed, sexual preference or their ability to pay for our services. Most importantly, we wanted it to be a safe space. We wanted our current residents and our graduates to be able to trust that they could come to the program at any time if they were in danger of relapse. We wanted to insure they would never again be forced to stay in living situations which presented a threat to them. And we believed the cornerstone of the program should be respect for the individual.

Today we know that a startling percentage of alcoholics are not only children of alcoholics, they are also co-dependents. Therefore, treatment is also provided to help our clients achieve a free, more independent style of thinking and living.

There are certain basic needs humans have, such as air, water, food, shelter and companionship. But when these basic human needs are made to apply to particular situations, they become wants disguised as needs. For example, one must have water to live, but one does not need water from a particular spring in a particular town in a particular country.

Similarly, a woman in need of companionship might decide that only a particular person can fill that need. She will do anything to have that person by her side. But if something happens to that person, is life over? Will there never be another to fill that need for companionship? It may feel that way, but it's almost never true.

This is not to say that it's addictive behavior to want someone or something. When the pursuit of that person or thing becomes one of the major obsessions of life, it can be called addictive behavior. Even this is not necessarily true addiction. For addiction to be present, one must be altered in some permanent way: physically, emotionally and spiritually.

Addictive Behavior Can Be Changed

So while addiction does not go away, addictive behavior can be changed. It's important to understand this point because it's probably the major difference between the thinking in the medical model and the addictions treatment programs in this country. What it means is once an addict always an addict. It doesn't mean that one is doomed always to drink, take drugs or eat uncontrollably; but it's necessary to keep the knowledge of one's addiction at the very center of one's attention on a daily basis. Only in this way can one frame one's lifestyle to meet the requirements for a user-free way of life.

Freedom From The Tyranny Of Addiction

What are those requirements? First and foremost, they include complete abstention from the addictive substance. Even in the case of food addicts, it's necessary to stay away completely from the items which trigger uncontrolled eating, not from not eating at all. The recovering addict must come to a clear understanding of this need, or she will not manage to stay clean, sober or abstinent. Indeed, in all cases where the addict returns to the use of her substance of choice, it will be because she hasn't understood the nature of addiction or because she decides to give in to it.

There is no such thing as bringing the addiction under control, being able to "use" socially or in moderation, or being able to live life well or to much real purpose while using.

Some years back a think-tank corporation published a report stating that alcoholics could return to moderate drinking if they refrained from using alcohol for a period of time and then reintroduced it into their lives in a slow and deliberate fashion. It was an interesting hypothesis, one from which a few alcoholics received a lot of comfort — until their addictions took over once again and left them suffering.

For alcoholics who take heart at such reports, their nearest bartender could have advised them as well. For the rest, they know that short-term gratification will never serve in the place of long-term fulfillment based on steady growth and acceptance of themselves as both alcoholic and worthwhile human beings.

The Toll Taken By Denial

Denial of addiction takes so many subtle forms it's difficult to sort them out. Some of the more obvious cases involve whole institutions such as research companies, the alcohol industry and the medical profession whose schools still teach so little about one of the major killers of people in this country. While rarely mentioned on death certificates, addiction is frequently the real cause of death in many people. It's a staggering number when we include automobile accidents, suicide and illnesses that were not treated in time because of active drinking.

The less obvious forms of denial involve individuals and families who, faced squarely with the problem, call it anything but what it is in an effort to avoid its consequences. Even people in recovery will confuse denial and feelings of boredom with their new lifestyles or with impatience with what they perceive to be their slow pace of progress in recovery.

Talk to someone in early recovery who is going through this denial and you'll probably hear her say that life is not what she expected; that she'd expected her family and friends would be more appreciative of her efforts. She'll probably tell you she thought situations in her life would have smoothed out more and that she should have begun to reacquire things that she lost while using. If she then goes on to say that her life is not better than when she was drinking, you can absolutely presume that she is still in denial of the reality of her addiction and what it did to her. Recovery is not about people, places and things changing. It's about recovery *inside* that leaves one able to handle the normal ups and downs of life.

Frequently families fall into this same trap, especially the man in the life of the woman addict. Very few significant others attend recovery groups after the women in their lives stop using. They seem to feel that once the drinking or whatever has stopped, they should then be able to handle whatever else comes along. Like many family members and friends of alcoholics, they believe once the drinking has stopped, all the problems that came with it will be cleared up as well. This kind of thinking doesn't take into account the fact that things at home were probably never right in the first place.

Alcoholism and drug dependence do not exist in a vacuum. They do not flourish in healthy ground. There are hundreds of thousands of cases in which family members, usually women, have taken steps to look at their own participation and unwitting assistance in the growth of the disease in their family group. Once they saw what they could correct about themselves, they stopped contributing to the illness and frequently the drinker reached for help also.

Jeannie's Story

Take the case of Jeannie and her husband:

Jeannie was 32 when I met her. She had a high school education with some college credits earned here and there in courses which interested her and was the mother of four children. Her husband was a businessman who functioned well in his work and as a provider, but had little time or interest in sharing feeling kinds of things.

Their children came into the world fairly close together. They were healthy and her pregnancies had been relatively uneventful. But Jeannie was tired and depressed from having too many babies in too short a time, without any help to speak of in the day-to-day work of raising them. She couldn't seem to stop her recurring bouts with bronchitis and pneumonia. Her pride would not allow her to admit she needed help to fulfill what she thought of as **her** responsibilities. So she kept on struggling, kept on falling ill and kept on getting more and more depressed.

She also became more certain there must be something fundamentally wrong with her because she felt such a deep sense of personal inadequacy. When she finally did find the relief that alcohol brought, it did not take her long to go through all the stages typical of alcoholism.

Meanwhile Jeannie's family continued to deny there was anything more wrong than Jeannie could put right if only she would stop that drinking. Her husband, who spent the most time with her, was divided about what was going on in their home. On the one hand, Jeannie seemed to be handling most things all right. She was content to be at home more which suited him fine since he had never cared much for socializing.

It was bothering him though that she did seem to be drinking more often. Every once in a while, she seemed to be worse than usual and would go on what he called "miniature binges." Those worried him! Nothing seemed important to her then and she did such irrational things.

Once he had come home from a meeting and had been unable to find her anywhere. Her car was in the driveway and the kids were safe in bed. She had never gone out and left them alone. He began to be frightened and started calling her. Just before he panicked, she answered from the bathroom. He went in and there she was, all of her clothes on, lying curled up in the dry tub. When he asked her what she was doing, she answered that the tub had looked so cool and appealing, she had lain down and fallen sound asleep. He was speechless at that and simply shook his head and walked away.

He never mentioned it again either. Instead he began to worry about her sanity. Still he continued to believe that things would change. He was sure that Jeannie, the woman he still loved deeply, would return to her senses.

What Jeannie's husband didn't know was that he too was changing. He was not just staying at home contentedly, he was trying to hide his home life from family, friends and co-workers. He worried constantly about his children and felt powerless to do anything to correct the situation, even if only for their sakes.

Although he prided himself on his faithfulness to Jeannie, he had to admit that other women were beginning to be more appealing and more interesting to him. Worst of all, he just didn't understand what was going on, so he felt frustrated and angry most of the time. His temper, never far under the surface, was always erupting at something.

Finally he began to try to control Jeannie's drinking. He hid her bottles and her beer; he tried spending more time with her; he cautioned the children to leave her alone, saying that she needed rest; he tried to think of diversions. Nothing worked. Instead, she actually seemed to get worse. He thought she must have started drinking even earlier in the day because no matter how early he arranged to come home, her eyes were always glassy and her speech was slurred. His heart was breaking but he didn't know what to do about it.

In the end, it was Jeannie's drinking that helped break his inertia and made him face the truth at last — his wife was an alcoholic. On that final evening, he had been puttering around his workshop while the kids played ball in the yard. Jeannie had headed for bed early, although he could hear her making frequent trips to the kitchen to get another drink. Around 8:30, while he and the kids were watching television in the living room, he got up to go to the kitchen and that's when he saw her. She was just leaning there in the doorway, only partially clothed, with this strange look on her face. Her eyes were swollen and she had a bruise on her chin. There was blood on her right hand where she was holding her side. The only thing he could think of was that she must have been attacked in the bedroom while he and the kids had been in the yard. His next thought was to prevent his children from seeing her but it was too late. They were already staring at their mother in horror, too frightened to move or say anything.

He took a few steps toward her, intending to help her back to the bedroom. That was when he knew that she had not been attacked — she was just terribly drunk. She misinterpreted his intentions and screamed at him to leave her alone, that she just wanted to get another drink. She tried to kick at him but lost her hold on the door frame in the process and started to fall. He caught her and picked her up at the same time and carried her quickly to the bedroom, roaring at the children to stay where they were and to be quiet.

Once in the bedroom, he put Jeannie on the bed and was amazed at how she kept trying to get up. Her one intention was to get past him to the kitchen where she kept her

supply. That was obviously how she had hurt herself in the
first place, by falling against things while trying to get out of
the room. Finally, after he had pushed her down half a
dozen times, she passed out.

He was worried that he'd really hurt her but she only
seemed to be asleep. He covered her with the blanket and
went back out to take care of the children. He told them
Mommy was just sick, that her fever had made her act
strangely. They didn't really believe it, but they wanted to
badly enough that they pretended to.

The next day Jeannie's husband finally told her what he
had so often thought of doing, but couldn't bear to do. He
gave her the choice of going to Alcoholics Anonymous or
getting a divorce. Having finally reached the end of his
ability to put off making that decision, he was almost as
willing to have one as the other.

In the language of Al-Anon, the self-help organization
for the families of alcoholics, Jeannie's husband had simply
been "enabling" her to go on drinking while she became
more and more ill, less and less able to cope with anything.
While his intentions had been good, he completely misun-
derstood the dynamics of what was happening and had
made a lot of wrong moves. Consequently, by the time he
did finally decide to give up trying to cure Jeannie himself,
he was also just about ready to give up on the marriage.

Unfortunately, he was not alone in his responses.
Approximately 90 percent of the husbands of alcoholics
are unable to bring themselves to participate in the treatment process, while the statistics are exactly the opposite
when it is the husband who is the alcoholic. It's small
wonder, therefore, that women wait so long before seeking treatment. The reality of having to deal with the double standard regarding women who drink to excess and
the awful self-loathing and fear of loss that accompanies
it is more than most women can bear.

Neither can they stop drinking on their own, so they
are caught in a Catch 22 that seems irreversible. While
Jeannie had some real issues to handle at this point, much
of what she was really feeling was self-pity. She had

passed the point in her disease where she could really feel much of anything that was not drug-affected and self-centered. Neither could her husband, for that matter. Although the actual drug-taking was done by someone else, he was feeling the effects too.

Both of them were caught in a downward spiral, full of self-hatred and resentment of each other. It would be irresponsible not to mention here that this is frequently the point in alcohol-affected relationships where the people involved reach for the wrong kind of help. Then more time is wasted while they sit on psychiatrists' couches, wading through the past and taking home prescriptions for the equivalent of alcohol in pill form. Too few doctors and psychologists are properly acquainted with the nature of alcoholism. Incredibly in this day and age few medical schools offer any courses in the treatment of alcoholics, let alone in the treatment of the disease as a family problem.

This couple was relatively lucky. The progress of Jeannie's illness had been so rapid that she had not suffered much physical or mental damage, certainly nothing irreversible. It was emotionally and spiritually that both she and her husband needed the most support and encouragement to pick up their lives and move on again.

In this respect, it was Jeannie who benefited most. Her husband's ultimatum turned out to be the best thing he could have done for her. Unfortunately he did not take his own advice, choosing instead to keep his feelings to himself in the belief that Jeannie was the only one with a problem.

If Jeannie's husband had known more about the disease of alcoholism, he would have learned that he needed his own support system in order to keep pace with the woman his wife was becoming. She continued to stay sober and to work on achieving an understanding of alcoholism and how it had affected her. He too needed to be willing to get in touch with the differing growth patterns which were separating them slowly and surely.

In the end, the gap between them was too wide to be bridged and the marriage ended in divorce. By that time, however, Jeannie at least was much better prepared to lead her own life in an independent way.

The other sad byproduct of their inability to work together on their recovery issues was that their children never found it either. Their mother was not able to help them with it at first and their father actively discouraged it since he felt it was only Jeannie's problem that needed to be dealt with then.

It's very important that children be included in any plans for recovery, whether it's addiction or co-dependence that is presenting the problem. Just as their lives are affected by their parents' dysfunction, so it will be changed by their recovery. The children will need to learn whole new ways of relating to each other and to their families. Their participation in everything — school, friendships, outside activities — will be different. Just as it's best for children to learn about fundamental things like religion, sex and the stresses of growing up from their parents, it's best that they learn about recovery from the people who are closest to them.

Co-dependence As Addiction?

Popular thought today says that co-dependency itself might be an addiction. I don't think so. It doesn't fit the classic definition of addiction, which is that one is addicted when his or her life is affected negatively in one or more ways because of the use of a chemical, sex, food, gambling or work. Nor does it fit the working definition I mentioned earlier which calls for the addicted to be affected in all of three ways: physically, emotionally and spiritually. The co-dependent can eventually be free of co-dependent behaviors if she is willing to work consistently for this freedom.

In actuality, I think co-dependent behavior relies on a set of well-defined patterns formed early in life which materially affect the context in which we live our lives. The bad news about these behavior patterns is that, left unchanged, they are progressive and eventually create disease in us. The good news is that, because they are learned, these behaviors can be unlearned and new, more healthy ones put in their places. This is not to say that such changes are easily made, however, since they go to the very root of the co-dependent's self-concept. It *is* possible to change one's self at depth and it's well worth the effort to do so.

The Enabler Co-dependent

The alcoholic needs at least one enabler. This is the person who essentially makes it all right for her to continue to drink. It's rare that the enabler knows she is filling this role, but it's a role that fits that person's need to be important to someone in a very fundamental way.

It may be the same person throughout the course of the alcoholic's life or it may be a series of people. It will always be a person who matches the addict in the need to feel good or to feel good about themselves.

For such a person, hope that the alcoholic will stop drinking not only springs eternal, just about anything inspires it. The alcoholic might take a pledge in church and go on the wagon for a while. The enabler co-dependent will take this as a sign that life will improve and indeed it does for a while. The alcoholic gets a job, is home at night, starts to feel better physically and begins to be available to the people around her. The enabler co-dependent will be happy about the changes for a while, until her self-concept begins to be changed by the emergence of the sober personality of the alcoholic.

When the alcoholic was drinking, the enabler co-dependent knew what was expected of her. Her role was clear, she felt worthwhile and needed. Unless she also receives treatment for her co-dependence, chances are excellent the relationship will disintegrate from the loss of its foundation.

An untreated co-dependent will certainly go on to reproduce her co-dependent relationship with another co-dependent.

Co-dependent enablers are every bit as much victims of alcoholism as the alcoholic herself. She cannot or will not admit the truth about its influence in her life. These are the people who, although surrounded by alcoholism in their families, continue to deny its presence. They are incredibly blind to what it has done to them and those around them. Their denial is a way to keep the fiction of normalcy alive.

Mrs. Reiser's Story

A typical enabler co-dependent is a woman we will call Mrs. Reiser:

As she went about preparing for dinner, Mrs. Reiser was thinking about her sister-in-law and about all the trouble she had caused lately. Alcoholics must just be weak people, she thought, and they must be lazy, too.

She remembered that man she passed on the street frequently who always tried to get her to give him a quarter. And once, while taking the Green Line home from shopping in Boston, she had seen a sight that completely disgusted her. This woman, although she didn't look like any woman Mrs. Reiser had ever known, had appeared on the train platform carrying two really full shopping bags. The creature had put the bags down beside one of the benches and proceeded to approach everyone there, asking for money. It made Mrs. Reiser shiver just to think about it.

Now, without even a "by your leave, ma'am," some agency was planning to use the old house across the street for a halfway house and for women at that.

That woman who had come around to invite Mrs. Reiser to an open house to explain the project hadn't fooled her in the least. The woman had tried to say she was an alcoholic, but she wasn't going to fall for that lie. She remembered the fights that took place in her brother's house when he had been married to his first wife. That woman was an alcoholic! Oh, she would stop drinking for a while sometimes, but she always looked terrible and was as nasty as could be. She couldn't be trusted either. Her drinking bouts seemed to start for no reason and they ended up in screaming fights, smashed furniture and usually somebody was hurt.

Mrs. Reiser could never understand how a beautiful young woman like her sister-in-law could become an alcoholic. She couldn't understand why she just didn't stop drinking. The girl was a college graduate, her husband was very much in love with her and they had two lovely children and a wonderful home. Finally her brother had been unable to stand it anymore. He had put his wife out of the house, bag and baggage. He said he wouldn't help her to drink herself to death anymore and that he would no longer be responsible for what happened to her.

The children had a hard time at first but their aunt helped out and they seemed to forget after a while, to adjust pretty well. She did worry about the youngest, though. He seemed always to be in one fight or another. But his big sister was wonderful. Never a peep out of her! She was just a perfect child. Her father was very lucky.

As a matter of fact, her brother was as lucky as their own father had been when their mother had got sick. It hadn't seemed like much in the beginning. Mother had just started having headaches and going to her room to rest after dinner. Then the time that she had spent in her room had seem to stretch until she had hardly ever come out.

Daddy had just said that everything would be okay, and that the children had to try extra hard to be quiet so Mother could rest and get well. The medicine her father brought to their mother never seemed to be enough to help her, but she really seemed to need it badly.

Mrs. Reiser had heard her mother late at night sometimes moaning and telling her husband that she couldn't wait, and that if he loved her, he would go get her some more. He always did and her mother seemed to feel better at last. At least she was quiet.

Mrs. Reiser wondered why she'd thought about her mother just then. There was certainly no connection between her poor sick mother and her lush of a sister-in-law. Her mother had been emotionally ill and immobilized because of it. Her sister-in-law was just wasting her life on booze and those prescriptions she was always getting.

No, she thought, alcoholics were just weak and lazy! They didn't deserve to be around ordinary people. They should put them away where they couldn't harm others.

She thought maybe they shouldn't even be allowed to get married and have children. Mrs. Reiser had heard there was a possibility that alcoholism might even be hereditary or that the tendency might run in families. Her poor niece and nephew, she sighed. They would really have to watch to see that they didn't mix in with the wrong kind of children.

The woman in the example here was steeped in denial. Anything or anyone who did not fit her conception of what was acceptable was cut out of her mind. She believed only what she chose to believe. No matter what the facts were, her mind was closed to any but her own rationalizations.

Her whole family was as co-dependent as it is possible to be. They sought each others' approval for their belief system and completely backed up whatever each other had to say. They created a self-perpetuating family system that had little real knowledge of the truth if it did not fit their preconceived notions.

There is little hope of growth or change in such a system. In a very real sense, they are spiritually starved. Even God would have to fit their beliefs, rather than the other way around. The result is that these people would always be settling for less.

CHAPTER 4

The Sexually Abused Co-dependent

The more unhealthy the home environment, the more seriously it will affect the children victimized by it. The more sensitive the children being raised in these poor environments, the more they will be affected.

This is exactly why some women who were sexually abused as very young children will sometimes cope with it by hiding it deep in their subconscious where the memory of it will be hidden from them, sometimes for many years.

A good example is the book *Sybil* by Flora R. Schreiber. Over years of abuse Sybil created multiple personalities whose job it was to protect her. It was their duty to cope with the horror of her victimization by a maniacal mother and an inept useless father. These personalities actually made it possible for Sybil to go on living in spite of enduring sustained and horrible torture. If that's not co-dependence, I don't know what is.

In other instances the value system instilled by their abusers prevents children from speaking about what goes on at home. Outsiders are portrayed as lacking in understanding and critical. Open criticism is feared by these children because it might hurt them and their abuser in some way. Having already had a portion of their personality formed, these children exhibit self-destructive behavior patterns because they feel responsible for the abuse and have begun to live at least a portion of their lives for someone else.

Some women simply block out any memory of having been abused until much later in life. When memory does return, it's usually greeted by the survivor with disbelief, then horror and finally acceptance. A great deal of support is needed all through the painful process.

Unlike the case of Sybil or those with blocked memory, if the abuse went on for a long time, it may be a very conscious memory. It will be the source of a great deal of anger, pain, anxiety, acting out and tragedy in later years.

Sara's Story

Sara's life is such an example:

The houses on her street rose three stories high. They were so narrow they seemed to have been glued together in order to keep them standing upright. They were unbearably hot in the summer; in winter even the mice left for a warmer climate.

Sara's family . . . her father, mother and her baby sister . . . lived on the top floor of 169 Winter Street. While it was old with peeling walls and was the last to get heat and water up through the building's old pipes, their apartment was all she had ever known.

Her mother was terribly thin and tired most of the time. She was the breadwinner of the family because her father spent most of his time drinking (or looking for a drink) in one of the neighborhood hangouts.

Sara's sister was four years younger and, at three, was barely out of diapers. When Sara was not in school, it was her job to take care of the baby until her mother arrived home from work around six in the evening. That way the babysitter could go home and her mother would not have to pay for extra time. Sara was just a baby herself, charged with the responsibility of caring for an even younger baby, but there seemed to be no other choice.

It was on one of these days when Sara was in charge that her father surprised her by coming home at four in the afternoon. He was not quite as drunk as usual. Instead of passing out on the couch, he sat watching the girls playing. He even tried joining in a few times but couldn't quite get into the game.

It felt strange to Sara because he had this funny look on his face and he kept watching her. She was glad when her mother came home. But she couldn't understand why her father had gone into the bedroom when he heard his wife coming in and had pretended to be asleep.

A few days later, he came in early again. Again he was only a little drunk, and he had brought a candy bar for her. She was even more puzzled this time but she was happy, too. In her child's way, she loved her daddy. She hated it when her mother talked about him in a mean way and she was frightened when her parents fought. She hoped that things were changing, and she wanted to make her father happy, happy enough to stay home and not to drink.

On the fourth or fifth time Sara's father came home in the afternoon, she and the baby were sitting on the floor in the living room, watching television. He sat behind them on the couch. When a commercial came on, he asked Sara to get him a glass of water from the kitchen. She jumped up, happy to please him. She brought back a nice full glass, carrying it ever so carefully so as not to spill it. He took it with a smile and patted his lap, beckoning her to sit on it. She was overjoyed to be asked. It was always the baby who sat in everybody's lap. It had been a very long time since anyone had even hugged her. Usually her mother was too busy and her father was too drunk.

Her father put his arms around her and started very gently rubbing her thigh and then the inside of her right leg. Sara was getting uncomfortable, but her daddy seemed happy and he was holding her very firmly with his left arm. Suddenly, he lifted her off his lap and put her on her feet

on the floor. Then he got up and walked quickly toward
the bathroom.

That afternoon was the beginning of the end of Sara's
childhood. Having had an orgasm from just touching his
daughter, he still convinced himself that Sara had not been
hurt. But addictions and obsessions always demand more
and more to satisfy them. After that day there were many
times when her father came home early and began to
fondle Sara. Eventually he took her into his bedroom and
encouraged her to touch him too. As she got older, he
introduced her to intercourse, assuring her all the time
that theirs was a special relationship and that they needed
to keep it to themselves.

This classic case of incest went on until she was 17.
Sara's father preyed upon her emotional starvation and
her mother seemed not to be able to see the signs.

As in many other kinds of child abuse, the perpetrator's
illness is confused and covered up by the alcoholism. Under its influence, he was able to justify and rationalize
the most outrageous behavior, leaving his other illness to
rage freely.

Sara was caught in a Catch-22 situation. During her
childhood her mother was overburdened and lacked the
will to fight back at life. She put up walls against everything, even her own children. Sara interpreted this behavior as meaning that she herself was unlovable.

When her father began to show affection, therefore,
she was confused. He, sensing this, built on her confusion,
trying to convince her that he was only doing what any
dutiful, loving father would do. Continuing to box her in,
he assured her that it was also her duty to take care of his
needs in her mother's place.

In order to insure secrecy, Sara's father made her promise never to talk about the real nature of their relationship.
He told her that her mother, her sister and others would
be jealous and angry with her. Somehow Sara knew that
wasn't the real reason, but her father was too powerful
and she was too afraid of the isolation she sensed she
would endure if she told.

So she kept the secret, kept on enduring the humiliation and became more and more sure that there was no way out for her. Even if there were, she reasoned, she was not worth anything. It was no wonder that Sara never felt truly comfortable with anyone, anywhere. She could never let down her guard to let anyone close enough to get to know her. She always felt like a phony. Sara was caught in a co-dependent relationship from hell.

When she was 17, Sara's ticket out of the house came through getting high. Once she discovered that magical feeling of being untouchable that booze and drugs gave her, she never wanted to be straight or sober again and she wasn't very often. She easily found friends who used as she did, and they quickly became very important to her. For one thing, they gave her the support she needed to make the break with her father. She left home to move in with one of her friends.

While Sara never went back home again, she was not able to break off with her father entirely. She didn't have sex with him, although he tried to convince her to "take care of him" on a few occasions when he came to visit her, bringing gifts of money and things she couldn't afford herself. Sara hated taking his presents and letting him visit, but she couldn't break the hold of the only person whom she felt had ever loved her and one who made her feel responsible for him.

Finally Sara met an attractive young man four years older than she. He was very different from her other friends and was nothing like her father. They soon found themselves falling in love and decided to get married and settle down. Sara was pregnant when they made their decision, but that seemed only to add to the rightness of it.

Unfortunately for their marriage, Sara was already suffering from alcoholism and drug addiction. She couldn't make any easy decisions about stopping her drinking or taking drugs.

For one thing, the awful pain from which she had sought oblivion originally was still there. Her husband, her marriage and her impending motherhood were able to ease it for a while, but she had no other way to cope. Neither marriage nor motherhood could offer anything but temporary escape.

With the beginning of her marriage, Sara entered a period of what is called "controlled" drinking. She was able to keep from having anything at all during her pregnancy by going out of her way to avoid any opportunity to drink. During this period, she dreamt a lot about getting drunk or high, thereby getting some help from her subconscious. She called these dreams "cheap drunks." She also cleaned the house a lot, she cooked and baked, she knitted, she painted the whole apartment. She did anything and everything which would keep her busy and away from the liquor store.

Her husband and their friends thought she was the most fantastic woman they had ever known. They never knew that what she was really doing was controlling her environment to the most extreme extent possible.

All the time she was pregnant, Sara hung on by thinking that the arrival of the baby would change everything. She wanted it so badly that she made herself believe it. Of course the baby's arrival didn't change anything.

Instead, Sara entered a period often described as a "dry drunk." That's a period when the very absence of alcohol in the addicted person seems to trigger the kind of behavior he or she exhibited while actively drinking.

In Sara's case, she became morose and withdrawn. She seemed to lose interest in everything that had meant so much to her, including her child. Everyone thought that she was just suffering from post-partum depression. Sara let them go on believing it because she was too ashamed to admit the truth.

To Sara, her wish to drink was proof of her inadequacy as a person. Having come from an alcoholic home, as well as one in which there was incest, the only way she knew how to deal with her pain was to drink. Therefore, every day that she didn't drink was to refuse herself the only relief she knew. She was always playing a role. She thought if people really knew her, they would not care for her.

Finally, the self-imposed isolation was too much. Two years after the birth of her first baby and just after having her second child . . . another daughter . . . Sara picked up her first drink in almost three years. It hit her like a ton of bricks.

Alcoholism is a progressive disease. Its degree is dependent on many factors, as is its rate of progress. That's why a person who has stopped drinking and picks it up again after a period of abstinence suffers from its effects even more than when he or she initially stopped drinking. Age, physical health, size, emotional and mental condition all play a part.

Sara was emotionally and spiritually drained from her long struggle to resist alcoholism on her own. Physically, she had not recovered from the pregnancy, nor from the lack of sleep or poor nutrition that followed. Within a very short time, Sara was back to drinking daily and it began to make a difference on the family budget. Fights were starting to happen over money. Sara responded by holding up payments on bills and using the money to buy liquor.

She started rationalizing her behavior with her first drink when she told herself that she deserved to have a drink now and again. She rationalized the non-payment of her bills in the same way. After all, her story went, they had a good credit record. She intended to pay; she was just slowing down a little. Didn't everybody do it? It would not have mattered what the situation was, she would have rationalized anything to get her supply and to protect it.

Her husband became more and more distraught. He was frightened to leave the children with her while he went to work. He was frightened of what was happening to his wife and he was frightened of what his life was now turning into.

After four years of trying to hold things together, hoping for a change, Sara's husband sued for a divorce using the grounds "Gross and Confirmed Intoxication." Sara countersued, charging mental cruelty.

After a particularly bitter court fight, Sara won her case and the children were awarded to her. Instead of improving, things became rapidly worse. Sara's now ex-husband could not stand the deterioration of his ex-wife and his children's lives, nor his powerlessness in the face of it, so he left the state to take a job 1,000 miles away.

Since her ex-husband stopped paying alimony when he moved, Sara went on welfare. She and her children began living with a series of disreputable characters, ostensibly to make the payments go farther, but really to make her drinking money last longer.

After Sara's first suicide attempt, made in the aftermath of a terrible binge, the State intervened on behalf of the children, removing them from Sara's custody temporarily. Because of the severity of Sara's drinking problem, they were sent to live with their father. Relieved of any restraints, even the minimal ones imposed by the children, Sara was free to do what she really wanted to do all along since that first day in the living room when her father had assaulted her.

She could now kill herself, slowly and with absolute hatred for herself, the life she had lived and the people in it. Every day of her life since her father had come home early so long ago had been part of a gargantuan effort to stay alive, not to give up, to keep on hoping that things would get better.

Now Sara began what was to become a series of visits to various institutions. When she botched a suicide attempt or was picked up for drunkenness and vagrancy, she was shipped off to one of the state mental hospitals or to a drug or alcoholism treatment center.

She actually seemed to be trying to get well in a few of these places, but she never let go of her secret agenda . . . taking her own life. Finally, during one of the in-between times, Sara got a job as an aide in a nursing home and was living in a studio apartment in one of the sadder sections of her city.

The day she finally chose as her last was not unusual in any way. She had started drinking early, around 10:30 a.m., just after getting home from work on the night shift. By mid-afternoon she was sitting at her kitchen table, staring at the wall. She had finished a fifth of gin and was starting on a second. She was not visibly drunk.

This was one of those times when she could not seem to get drunk, no matter what. Instead she became more and more morose, haunted by her past and refeeling all the old anger and self-loathing.

Finally she got up, went into the kitchenette and took the long carving knife out of the drawer. She went back to the table, putting it down carefully, just as she had handled that glass of water for her father that day long ago.

Then she went to get the phone from the end table. She brought it back, put it beside the knife and her bottles of gin and sat down again. She looked down at herself, noted her white uniform and thought that its representation of purity was very fitting to that moment.

Having at last reached an absolute zero in all of her personal resources, Sara picked up the phone and called a man whom she had been seeing off and on during the past few years. He was much older than she, much closer to her father's age. He also was an alcoholic. He was always going on the wagon, only to slip off again whenever he thought he had a good enough excuse. He was always ready to listen to a tale of woe from a fellow drunk, especially Sara. He had even known her father and sometimes he felt as if she were his daughter too.

On this day when he answered the phone, she talked to him for a few minutes about nothing much. Then while he was speaking, rambling on as she had induced him to do, Sara picked up her knife. Quickly, cleanly and with great force and determination, she brought it up to her neck and cut her jugular vein. While her body was still numbed by shock, she dropped the knife, held her free hand over the wound and told the man what she had just done. In her final act of bitterness and cruelty, which she could not even then bring herself to direct at her real father, she asked him to talk to her until it was over.

Sara's way of dealing with her situation was unusually extreme. The events which led up to it, however, were not unusual. The latest statistics show that female children are sexually molested at a rate of one out of four. More and more often women who have been victims of this crime are showing up in treatment for drug and alcohol abuse. One of the sadder aspects of all this is that the emotional damage is so great, that recovery sometimes takes too long a time for its victims.

Co-dependent Adult Daughters Of Dysfunction

Women have gone almost to the 21st century without having achieved nearly enough advancement with respect to their development as full partners with men in the world. I believe this is evidence itself of dysfunction in the human family and that women are its chief victims. Women form co-dependent relationships generation after generation with men who are the authority figures in their lives. Their children inherit this dysfunction. Then they in turn hand it on to *their* children and so on.

In a home where active addiction is present, there is certainly no such thing as equality, only dysfunction and all it brings with it. The context in which the family lives its life together is *dis-ease*. The disease of the alcoholic parent is visited upon all members of the family.

It's no wonder that children of dysfunction learn how to be co-dependent so well. It's the only way to survive in

that strange world. Alcoholics who are still drinking are
dependent on an inorganic substance. By its nature that
substance can neither think nor feel nor respond to its
user. Yet it induces abuse and then goes on to punish
those unfortunate enough to be caught by it.

It's important to note that dependence and co-dependence are different coping mechanisms. Passing on to their
children what they know so well, active alcoholics teach
dependence . . . on people, places and things. They will
use anything which will change the way they feel, rein-
force their perceptions of the world or relieve them of the
responsibility for their actions. Someone, however, must
accept that responsibility. That usually means the brunt
of the alcoholic's actions fall on the co-dependent people
closest to him or her.

It's a statistical fact that the majority of alcoholics are
men (although the gap is becoming less wide than it has
been in the past) and that there is usually at least one
woman around him whose job is to counterbalance him.
Adult Children of Alcoholics (ACoA) meetings and therapy groups, therefore, are largely filled with women, as
are Al-Anon meetings. It seems clear then that women
are still standing in for the alcoholic male at home.

The woman is still more often victimized by incest and
physical, sexual and psychological abuse. When she leaves
one household, she will be moving into a new life with
another person. If she has not dealt with her co-dependence issues, chances are that the only kind of person she
will be able to form a partnership with will be similar to
the alcoholic parent with whom she formed her primary
relationship.

History teaches us that the past is prologue to the future
and that those who do not learn from their mistakes are
bound to repeat them. This is why the adult child who does
not receive help for her co-dependency can only repeat the
unhealthy family system which gave her life. If we know
no differently, the worst of conditions will seem normal to
us. Attitudes become hardened and resentments internalized for so long create personality changes in people which

can take a lifetime to undo. Fear, free-floating in the alcoholic family system, becomes a sickness of its own.

The safest way to cope is to please everybody if possible or at least the key players. In pursuit of this goal, children of alcoholics become chameleons, adapting themselves to their surroundings. At best, they learn to become almost anything; at the least, they learn not to offend.

These examples represent two extremes, of course, so they are not that difficult to spot. More difficult to see are the adult children who are in the middle of the spectrum. They can hide their dysfunctional histories from others better, and more importantly, from themselves.

The Family Matrix

My dictionary *(Funk & Wagnalls Standard College Dictionary,* 1974) defines a matrix as being that in which anything originates, develops, takes shape or is contained. It then goes on to list ten ways in which matrix is used to define different functions, ranging from the anatomy up to and including printing. Interestingly, the very next word listed in my dictionary is "matron," which is defined as being a "married woman who is usually a mother." Both matrix and matron come from the Latin noun "mater" or "matris" meaning "mother."

In today's society, the mother is still the matrix of the family system. The truth, however, is that the family itself, be it the immediate family or the larger family represented by society, is the mold for the personalities that emerge from it.

Today we know that we cannot blame "Mom" for everything that goes wrong in her child's life. Instead it's the family system that must take *responsibility* for the behavior patterns each child forms in order to deal with whatever comes along. Ultimately, these patterns form the foundation of the life of every individual.

Let's go back to the dictionary now for the definition of *responsibility.* Funk and Wagnalls says it is the state of being answerable legally or morally for the discharge of duty, trust or debt. Our society, from the Federal government on down through Mom and Pop, is supposed to share the *responsibility* for the quality of life for the people in it. When we examine it, however, does our society really take that *responsibility*? For that matter, does it work at all for women and for their children?

I don't think so and we do not need to go into a complete sociological treatise to prove it. It's easy to see that women have been especially hard hit by society's failure to be responsible to them individually and as a group. Society neither protects, encourages nor affirms women. Just taking a surface look, we see . . .

- That today almost half of all marriages end in divorce and that afterward women suffer a substantial loss in their standard of living while most men improve theirs within a few years.
- That the majority of women work at hard, unsatisfying and low-paying jobs that offer little chance to get ahead.
- That when they enter professions, women still tend to go into service work, which allows them greater flexibility for the purpose of raising their children, but leaves them fairly expendable in the job market.
- That when women do stay home to raise their children, they frequently find that life, society and their husbands have left them behind when the child-rearing time is at an end.
- That women will represent the largest group living below the poverty line by the year 2000 — and their children will be with them.
- That the vast majority of women are locked in a co-dependent relationship with society, the depth of which is only beginning to be understood.
- That minority women, including blacks, Hispanics, Asians, lesbians and new immigrants, have several extra strikes against them when it comes to getting

fair treatment in areas of jobs, housing, child care and education.

The matrix for society, the family, needs thorough re-examination. Corrective action must be taken if we are to unlock the chains that keep all of us bound to each other in such an unhealthy, anti-growth system. New definitions must be constructed concerning what a family is. In a highly mobile and technically oriented society like ours, the concept of an extended family has all but disappeared. We need to bring it back in such a way as to enrich and enlarge each person's experience.

Jeannie's Story Continued

Bringing it into human terms so that we may focus on the problem more clearly, let's look at the story of Jeannie again.

In addition to being an alcoholic, Jeannie, whom we met earlier, is also a co-dependent.

Her father had been an authoritarian person whose temper was never far below the surface. While he was fairly tame when sober, he was loud and frightening when he had been drinking too much. He was not a frequent drinker, so the family never knew when he would arrive home drunk. Therefore they were always apprehensive in the evening, waiting for the sound of his voice, listening for the tell-tale thickening in his speech and watching for the stagger in his walk.

It was on those drinking nights that Jeannie learned about fear, the fear that would serve to control her for a long time. Not that he ever hit her. He did not need to because the threat was there, every bit as real as if he smashed her with his hand. Jeannie had seen the bruises on her mother, and she had seen him beat her brother. It didn't seem possible that he wouldn't violate his own strange code which called for him never to strike his daughters.

Jeannie's mother was as afraid of her husband as the children were. She saw herself as powerless against his strength and helpless to do anything different, given her

economic situation. Like her mother before her, Jeannie's
mother saw herself in something of a trap. She had more
children than she could hope to support adequately. She was
cut off from her family because of geographical distance and
she saw herself as the one responsible for keeping her
family together.

On her father's side, Jeannie's grandparents were
immigrants, had never received much schooling and saw
their son as their best chance to move ahead in the world.
They pampered him and catered to him, and saw his wife as
a very ordinary woman who was a poor match for a son
who had so much to offer. Consequently, Jeannie's in-laws
gave her no support whatsoever. They actually undermined
her with her husband and with her children whenever the
opportunity arose.

In the home she had been raised in, it was Jeannie's
grandmother who had been the dominant parent. She had
set the tone for the family's lifestyle. She had denigrated her
husband and had pushed Jeannie's father to succeed,
tying him to her very tightly in the process. Clearly, she had
been the primary relationship in Jeannie's father's life.

As you can see, this family matrix encouraged isolation
even across generations. Fear and control formed the
gluey strands that held Jeannie's family together. No one
took the responsibility to ensure quality in the lives of the
family members. Everyone had to learn to shift for themselves as well as they could. Escape from that painful
reality had been possible only through alcoholism. Even
moving far away had not helped the individual family
members because they'd stayed a part of the family matrix
and took it with them wherever they went.

Things might have turned out very differently for Jeannie if anyone close to the family had taken responsibility for
calling her parents to account for the way they were handling their home life. But there was no one to do that. Not
their church, which was so big that it didn't really know its
members, not friends who felt it was none of their business,
not social workers and certainly not family members.

Think what might have happened if Jeannie's had been an extended family and the members had decided to do an intervention on her father. When he had to be *responsible* for his behavior, her father might have acted very differently. Even if he had not changed, the family might have made decisions which would have made it possible for the rest of the family to carry on without him. His children might then have had the opportunity to grow in a healthy way.

I'd like to make it clear here that I'm not talking about government intervention. I'm talking about people of good-will trusting themselves and one another to bring about good outcomes in spite of the difficulties involved. The barriers we've erected against so called "outside" help ought to be taken down to allow light and air in on our closed family sub-groups.

Our matrices need re-examination to allow more creativity in searching for answers to seemingly insolvable problems.

For instance, so many children waste away in orphanages or temporary foster care. They are too old, are from minorities or have too many problems for most Mom and Pop families. So society shifts them around until they are old enough to dump out on the street. After that, it's a matter of luck or fate as far as what happens to them. Yet there are lots of people who are willing to adopt these children and give them a positive start in life. The reason they are turned down is because they do not live "traditional" lifestyles. It seems unforgivable to me to waste our resources especially when it means that our children are being wasted as well.

Until recently in Massachusetts lesbians or gay men were not allowed to provide official foster care homes for any of the 25,000 children on the Welfare rolls. They may still only do it when the case worker considers it appropriate, which is not to say that it was not done unofficially before. Exercising their rights, parents who had no faith in the State's social services system simply made private arrangements with women and men whom they trusted to care for their children appropriately, thus by-passing the system altogether. I know of several such cases in which loving and nurturing people helped women to care for their children when they could not, returning them to their mothers eventually in better shape than when they were received.

On the other hand, I know of several cases where children were placed with nonsupportive relatives by the child welfare people who showed their bias against the birth mothers by ignoring her needs or working against her. This is one of the reasons that case reviews in Massachusetts are supposed to be attended by an independent and hopefully objective member of the community in which the children's mother lives. It is better than nothing, but that still amounts to only two hours of community supervision every six months.

The following two cases both involve women who had been sentenced to prison for drug-related offenses:

In the first, the mother sought the help of two women who had been in a mutually supportive and loving long-term relationship to care for her young daughter. The women cared for and nurtured that child until the mother was ready to take her back.

In the second case, the woman agreed to have relatives in another State care for her baby son until she was released from prison. This woman not only completed her incarceration, she completed a six month drug treatment program, went to work and got herself a place to live. But the relatives she trusted never expected her to succeed in her rehabilitation and refused to return the child to his mother, and were aided in their refusal by the laws in their own state. Five years later, she is still fighting for her child.

CHAPTER 6

The Primary Relationship

The person who exerts the most control over a child in the formative years constitutes the primary relationship in that child's life. Some people believe the child's mother, since it is usually she who spends the most time with the child, constitutes this primary relationship. While it can be so, of course, it is not always so.

Necessary Components

Actually, three things seem to be necessary to the formation of the primary relationship, each as important as the next:

1. *Access:* Having free access to the child means that the adult's will can be worked on the child without the restraints that lack of time could bring to bear.

One of the chief complaints of prisoners of war in Vietnam was that their captors could keep them for interrogation or punishment for as long as they wanted. They interrupted their sleep, fed them only when they wished and generally wore them down so that they would say or do anything in order to be let alone, if even just for a little while.

This treatment was to prepare the prisoners for the brainwashing that would follow. Imagine how much easier the job would be if they were working with children who had not yet formed opinions, learned to differentiate between ideals nor learned that some people are not to be trusted.

2. *Authority:* In a child's life, anyone tall enough for the child to look up to is an authority. Adults are big and strong and can back up their threats. They can withhold basic survival needs, such as food and water, sleep and physical security. They can also withhold love, approval, support, freedom and happiness and prevent others from providing them. They directly affect the quality of that child's life. Parents, guardians and sometimes siblings can have absolute power over young children.

When one of my sons was only four years old, I took him to the laundromat with me. He was standing beside me as I folded the clothes I had washed and I became aware that he was staring at an older woman of about 70, with very white hair and lots of wrinkles. She was sitting quietly waiting for her wash to be finished. She was aware of my son looking at her, but probably thought he would stop soon. However my son stared so long that both the woman and I became uncomfortable. Finally she spoke to him . . .

"Hello, little boy, how are you?"

My son said, "I'm fine." Then with a big breath he took advantage of the opening she had given him and asked, "You're old, aren't you?"

Surprised but game, the woman said, "How old do you think I am?"

My son continued to stare and seemed to be studying the woman very intently before answering. Finally he asked politely, but very seriously, "Fourteen?"

The woman was charmed and I was very relieved. I don't even remember if she told him her actual age but it didn't matter.

Even at the age of four my son knew about adults. He knew that he should be polite because this woman had the authority of all adults. However, he didn't know how to fit this woman into his frame of reference. She was a great deal older than the adults in his experience and 14 seemed a huge number to him. His curiosity forced him to grapple with the problem of defining this authority figure.

3. *Power:* The people who bring them food, soothe fears or offer happiness or a feeling of being special wield power over children. Young children cannot differentiate between the people who really meet their needs and those who only pretend to. Anyone who is bigger and stronger than another has potential power over that person. What separates people is the way they use their power.

Another of my sons was an absolute dynamo of happy energy when playing with his friends but he was very shy and timid with adults he did not know. He had a wonderful teacher in first grade who he really loved and who I believe returned his affection. I will bless that lady all the days of my life because she knew that my son's transition to second grade would be difficult because of his attachment to her.

In order to ease the way for him, she actually took him to visit the second-grade teacher, explaining that she was a friend of hers and that he would be very happy in that class too. By giving him this extra attention, my son's teacher let go of him in a very

professional way and introduced him to the continuum of school.

The Growth Of The Primary Relationship

The socialization process begins with babies and is continued and reinforced at every stage in a child's development. Through it people learn to conform to the norms
and the standards of their community. The community is
very small in the beginning of life. It only begins to expand
as the child grows older and is able to include others as
members of that community. The access to the child, which
is so great during the early years, exaggerates and magnifies
the power and authority of the child's immediate family.

As a result children pick up all kinds of signals from the
people around them. They always interpret them with
regard to what will provide them with the greatest margin
of safety. Therefore, if one parent is not present much,
the child will automatically look to the other to have its
needs met. If one parent is aloof and unresponsive to the
child's need for love and affection, the child will turn to
the parent or other significant person who seems willing
to meet those needs. If one parent is unassertive and
withdrawn from decision-making concerning the child,
the child will look to the other parent for permission to do
things. Each time the child seeks permission or affection
or the companionship from an authority figure and those
things are forthcoming, that person's power grows in the
eyes of the child.

With female children, more than with males, words are
not as necessary for them to understand what is expected.
They are taught from the beginning in their observations
of their mothers to tune into what others want or need.
As a result, their self-worth will be drawn from what
they interpret to be the approval or disapproval of the
primary figure in their life. Therefore, she'll be easily
manipulated for the ends of that person. At this early
stage of her development, her ability to be sensitive to the

people around her begins to be subverted to the needs of others. Instead of being the incredibly valuable tool it should be, it's used against her and later it's devalued for the very reason it's so useful.

We'll go back again to our earlier example to help explain further just how the process works. In Jeannie's family, her father seemed to control everything, the family revolving around him when he was present. But it was her mother who really set the pattern of her children's lives.

She and her husband had a co-dependent relationship which was based on their need for the mutual emotional security they could give each other within the context of their marriage. Jeannie's mother saw her job as that of being at home, available to her husband when he returned there. And he always did come back, regardless of how many affairs he might have had along the way. But during his absences his wife led her own life, developing friendships and pursuing her own interests. Things were so different when their father was home that his children came to look upon those occasions as time out from their regular life.

Jeannie's father and mother fought a lot about his affairs and about his neglect of his family but they never seriously entertained the idea of breaking up. Neither of them really wanted any other lifestyle than the one they had. Although they didn't realize it consciously, they could not conceive of being married to anyone else. They'd found in each other a person who would provide them with emotional security and protection from ever having to grow up.

Jeannie, having learned at her mother's and father's knees the mechanisms of co-dependency, would follow that same path in her own life. Jeannie's mother was the only person she could depend upon to be around when she was needed. She kept the family going and provided all the emotional security that was to be had. From her, Jeannie learned that men were not to be trusted or valued very much and that the best she could hope for from a marriage was to be left alone.

She also learned that it was important for her to be
tuned into the needs of others if she were ever to see that
her own needs would be met. Later, when she chose a life
partner, her conscious choice was a person different from
her father. Subconsciously, she was looking for someone
who would give her approval or at the very least would
not disapprove of her.

Reproducing The Primary Relationship

As we have seen, Jeannie was bound to her mother in a
very deep co-dependent relationship. She learned eventually
to reproduce her mother's life patterns, although she would
never have admitted it then. Indeed, the learning was unconscious and her choice disguised by surface differences.

Like her mother, Jeannie married a man who separated
himself from the daily life of his family by becoming involved in his own pursuits. His work or his workshop
projects took the place of the affairs her father had involved himself in regularly. Jeannie was solely responsible
for the upbringing of their children and she, too, developed
friendships and outside interests to cope with her loneliness. Like her mother, Jeannie was an alcoholic, having
turned to alcohol in her early 30s, at the peak of her feelings of frustration with her life.

The important thing to note here is that previously, in
generation after generation, Jeannie's family had continued the same co-dependent patterns. Co-dependent people reproduce co-dependent relationships over and over
because they have come to believe there is no other way
for them to function. Only when they see how these
relationships actually retard the growth of the individuals
in them, *can* they *change* them. Only when they can see
that these kinds of relationships actually victimize the
parties by keeping them tied to the past do they become
willing to change them.

In the meantime, people aren't static; they cannot stand
still. If they're not recovering, if they're not moving for-

ward, if they're not changing and growing, then they are moving backward. They are becoming less and less healthy and more unable to act in their own best interests.

We see this kind of effect all the time in families where poverty keeps them stuck in nonproductive, self-defeating lifestyles. Parents in these situations feel hopeless and unequipped to move on with life. They haven't got the strength or the resources to guide their children to a more positive way of life. So the children, too, become mired in the same quicksand as their parents.

The "I've Got Mine, And You Can't Have Any" Syndrome

One of the unfortunate truths about life in this country is what I call the "I've Got Mine, And You Can't Have Any," or IGMAYCHA syndrome. During our history, everytime there has been an influx of immigrants because of some major world event . . . the famine in Ireland, world wars, slavery in the South, pogroms in Russia . . . the people already established here (who were also immigrants at one time) tried hard to keep these newcomers out. If that wasn't possible, they tried to relegate them to the status of nonpersons, to keep them outsiders.

In response, and until they are really assimilated, these immigrants and their descendants invest themselves in ethnic pride, forming clubs or churches together, occupying whole neighborhoods where they keep their traditions alive. When they have evolved to the point of establishing neighborhood bases, then the rest of the people in the world are outsiders.

Eventually these societies work against allowing any of their own to break out of the community. For anyone among them to succeed is equal to refuting the community and being disloyal to it. The escapee then becomes an outsider also.

What does all this have to do with women? They are the ultimate outsiders of all times. They occupy the bottom rung of our hierarchical ladders. And it seems everything conspires to keep them there. Back in the '70s when women were getting together in small groups to talk to each other, it was considered a very radical and threatening thing to do. Why? Because women who talk to each other about real feelings and about the way things are in their lives are no longer isolated and alone.

Today it's still the one thing women need to do more of to gain a perspective on themselves and their lives. It's an extremely helpful way to learn about oneself as a woman. It's an important way to come to respect what being a woman means. Coming to like and love other women is the one sure path to learning to love oneself.

Religious And Racial Co-dependence

Interestingly, there are whole traditions formed around co-dependent behaviors. Religious traditions, for example, require children to be brought up in the parents' faith. It doesn't matter that the children might have their own ideas. For all intents and purposes, they are owned by their parents' religion. Then those same children must marry only others of their religion and bring up their children in it also.

As enlightened as we like to think we are in the United States, the same kinds of strictures apply with regard to race. Not only are people within the racial group discouraged from pairing outside it, people on the outside also create pressures to keep them from doing so.

How about people who push their children toward certain professions in order to enhance or maintain their own self-images? In the process, value judgments are made that are passed on through the generations, taking on the force almost of law.

It's easy to see that co-dependent behavior affects us at just about every level of human development, both in the community and in the family structure.

Hitting Bottom

What is "hitting bottom?" Is it different for non-addicted co-dependents? How does it affect women in particular?

I define hitting bottom as that point at which there is an overloading of our spiritual and emotional and physical faculties to the extent that we can no longer continue to live as we had been. Our old coping mechanisms have stopped working, and we have reached a point of surrender. It is a time of both confusion and relief because somehow we know that the fight is over but we don't know what comes next.

When that incredible moment when we bottom out arrives, it can be tumultuous. It may include anguished tears, anger and pain. For others the moment comes quietly with a soft sigh of recognition of our truth. It's always memorable! We never forget where we were or what we were doing at the time.

Judy's Story

The following experience is typical.

It had been an awful night. We had screamed and yelled, and he had got very drunk. Before he finally passed out and I had curled up on the couch to sleep, a lot of our things were broken by both of us. The apartment was a mess!

When I woke up the next morning, I felt completely awake and alert. Immediately the thought came to me that something new was happening to me. I became aware that I felt completely peaceful. It was a brand new feeling to me. There had never been a time in my life when I felt as relaxed and at ease as I did now. Instinctively I knew that I would live my life differently from that time on, even though I did not know how I would accomplish the change. I also knew that while I still hoped he would, it didn't matter whether or not my husband decided to join me in making this change.

Reaching bottom means we can no longer ignore the spiritual sickness that eventually keeps life from being worth living. Those of us who reach this point know we can't tell one more lie. We can't put aside one more of our values. We can't continue to settle for less. We can't live one moment longer with our loneliness. We must do something. We must not be alone any longer with our self-hatred and our hopelessness.

It's while experiencing this feeling of surrendering that some people have reported undergoing religious conversions or decided to return to church after having been absent for a long time. Still others reach for therapeutic intervention or support from family and friends.

Fortunately today there are many self-help groups all over the country which can offer us help. They range from Alcoholics Anonymous up to and including Co-dependents Anonymous. They make it possible for people with similar concerns to come together to help one another. Peer support which is specific to the recovery concern is often the best kind of help.

There are also many aware therapists, both male and female, who have come to understand the needs of the recovering person. Many people in self-help groups also see a therapist regularly as a way to optimize the support and guidance available to them. It constitutes the best of all possible worlds for healing from co-dependence and other dependencies and addictions.

Whatever the choice each individual makes when reaching for help, the period following bottoming out will be a time of extreme vulnerability. This is especially true when it becomes apparent that our old coping mechanisms are no longer working in a practical, day-to-day sense.

We'll experience a constant challenge to return to our negative thinking, our old habits, old behaviors or addictions. In spite of all the things against it, we'll be subject to a kind of insanity that will push us to act against our own best interests and return to the lifestyle we know so well. It doesn't even matter what we'd be returning to. Since we've always been able to rationalize living with it in the past, we could convince ourselves to do it again. This urge to give up is justified with statements like,

"The devil you know is better than the devil you don't know." Fear of the unknown is a powerful force against change, no matter how terrible the reality of our lives.

The habit of rationalizing and making excuses can easily combine with our old enemy, *procrastination,* until we come to understand that *feeling better* is far from being the same as *getting better.* While the principle is very simple, learning to change the ground rules we live by is the hardest thing we will ever do. Fortunately for our resolve, it's also the most worthwhile.

CHAPTER 7

Drawbacks For Co-dependent Women

We see this powerful fear of the unknown at work in the cases of women who are physically abused at home, have the perpetrator arrested, but then refuse to press charges. Certainly they fear retaliation, but they are also afraid to be alone; afraid that no one else will want them; afraid that they cannot support themselves and their children. They are afraid, afraid, afraid!

Like our addict sisters, nonaddicted co-dependent women wait far too long to go for treatment. They're afraid of society's disapproval of women who don't stay at home being quiet, keeping the home together and buying society's view that they are somehow less if they do not choose to do so.

How often have women been cautioned to make sure that they take care of their mates because there is always another woman out there waiting to take over? There's some basis in truth for this warning. When the stakes are high enough or some advantage is to be gained, women feel they can't afford to take care of each other. But how could they do any different, given that they are taught how powerless they are and how fearful they need to be and how insecure in the face of their helplessness? This is the way women are socialized in a patriarchal society. If they act in any other way, they alter that society's control over them too much and new rules must be developed to keep them in their places.

It's because of these built-in forces against change that it's so important for women to have knowledgeable help available. When they're ready to let go of their old ideas and reach out for something better, they will undoubtedly be ready for some kind of treatment. The type and duration of this treatment will vary with the individual, with the area of the country she lives in and in many cases, unfortunately, with how much money she has available. The difficulty involved in finding help should not be an excuse not to look for it.

Treatment Directions

When looking for treatment, there are some important things to take into consideration. There are three main factors which may or may not present themselves as neatly as the following examples. Because I don't believe a person who is suffering physically can make much use of any psychological help until she has mended, I will start with that.

Physical Health

Addicts

Co-dependence and chemical dependence have very different requirements at the beginning of recovery. The physical condition of the addict may call for medical attention initially. If not, there is still a period of at least six weeks that must pass before the effects of the alcohol and/or drugs she has ingested have worn off. At least that's the medical model designed for treating men in recovery. I believe it takes women longer.

The latest information on women alcohol users explains that the enzymes in their stomachs cannot break down alcohol as efficiently as those of men. That means that substantially more alcohol, which is literally a poison, is released into their bloodstream when they drink. Over time the cumulative effect on women's bodies and brains is naturally greater than the effects on most men.

Based on this information, it makes sense that women's bodies must also take longer to repair themselves. Indeed, this observation has been made by many who work with recovering alcoholic women.

This factor was important to the program we designed for Serenity, Inc., the recovery program for women that I co-founded in 1974. It included at least three months for rest and gradual reintegration into the outside world. During that time, we saw that all medical and dental needs (an amazing variety) were met. Meanwhile our clients learned various self-supportive living skills like cooking and cleaning, eating regular meals and resting and sleeping for appropriate amounts of time each day. In other words, we helped our residents learn how to nurture themselves.

If you are alcoholic or drug dependent, or if your problems have included some form of physical debility, it would be a good idea to seek medical help when beginning recovery. Your own doctor would be a good place to begin finding out about medical treatment. Although the unfortunate truth is that most medical schools offer little training on addictions, a doctor will certainly recognize and treat any individual health problems.

The bitter joke among doctors who've become aware of the need for more training in treating addictive people is that their education regarding addiction was of the "four-two-one" variety. That is, they attended four years of medical school and received two hours of lecture on the number-one health problem in the United States.

Non-addicted Co-dependent Women

Co-dependent women who are not alcoholics or drug addicts may also need this initial period of physical renewal. This is especially true if they were victims of physical or emotional abuse in their relationships or, just as importantly, their own self-neglect.

Women who may need still a different kind of medical assistance might include anorexics, bulimics, overeaters or people who have abused themselves in some particular addictive way. It's of primary importance to pay attention to the needs which present themselves early in treatment.

To begin taking care of oneself is also an important part of recovery. As women we've been socialized to think of ourselves as the care givers. We're taught that our needs are not only secondary to those of others, but should be met only when we have taken care of everyone else. As a result, women have frequently neglected themselves in all sorts of ways . . . ways that we would never have thought of neglecting others. There are few women reading this who don't know what I mean.

A Dream For Tomorrow

All of the clients in the Serenity program were addicted to alcohol or drugs or both. As far as I know there are no long-term treatment programs for nonaddictive co-dependents, although I can certainly see a need for them. It seems like a heavenly dream to think of a long-term recovery program for co-dependent women. It would be one that would encourage her to rest and recuperate. It would help her to think of herself first for a little while. And it would help her reconnect with the significant people in her life so she could put her relationships with them on a more fulfilling basis.

Emotional Health

The purpose of recovery is to enable us to put our lives into balance and to *keep* them there. This cannot be done unless there is emotional growth. The beginning of recovery is the start of a truly amazing balancing act which will continue for the remainder of each person's road back to health. If our physical well-being suffers, so will our emotions. If we are out of whack emotionally or mentally, we're likely to suffer physically.

When we think about it, it becomes clear that when people are controlled as tightly as co-dependents (addicted or not) are from the earliest periods of their lives, our emotional growth must have been stunted. At one extreme, we've been able to experience emotion only in reaction to the emotions of our controllers. On the other hand, we have resisted consciously experiencing any emotion at all.

In either case, someone else was pulling our strings, jerking us here and there like puppets. The result was that instead of maturing emotionally . . . growing up . . . we just grew taller. As children in adult bodies, the more we were called upon to participate in life on life's terms, the more we suffered from feelings of inferiority and loss of self-esteem. We felt like phonies and were always in fear that someone important to us would discover our charade.

Later we attempted to change our lives by changing the way we felt. Our paths took us through the use of any number of escape mechanisms, all the way from alcoholism through food or other addictions, bad relationships and finally for some, suicide attempts.

In recovery, it becomes apparent that emotional health is attained by following a difficult road which will include taking a hard look at ourselves. We need to examine the patterns of behavior which led us to near self-destruction in the first place. This is always a painful process and should never be attempted alone. Nor should it be undertaken with such abandon that the recoverer is brought to the brink of disaster again.

Timing Is Important

My advice to substance abusers, food addicts and women with strong negative behavior tendencies, is to postpone co-dependency and adult child issues until balance and sobriety have been practiced as a way of life for at least a year. I say this even though I know that there is a strong pull for these people to deal with everything as soon as possible.

Experience tells me that unless a firm foundation has been laid for sobriety, anything too heavy to handle can push over the recovering person. The danger is that if she goes back to her addiction or retreats into anorexic or bulimic behaviors again, she may not survive to get back to work on her issues.

It is never a path to freedom to give in to the kind of destructive self-will that brought them down in the first place. I say this even though I know that with respect to alcoholism, some people think it is a weakness to be un- able to drink again. I say that when a person who has suffered so much at the mercy of a substance that has neither heart, soul nor compassion for its user, thinks that the goal for him or her is to drink again, that person is slipping toward lunacy.

Emotional health is only built by facing life the way it is. It deals with reality. Reality as a way of life has been thoroughly lacking in the lives of people who are into our diseases. Both physical and emotional health must be firmly planted in spiritual health if we are to grow and flower in the way necessary to support a healthy lifestyle.

Spiritual Health

Spirituality is the glue that holds us together as indi- viduals and puts us together again if we do start to come apart.

When we stop looking to other people or to ourselves alone for our answers, we will have cleared the way for help from a power greater than ourselves.

This is precisely the time when we become able to stop living alone with our fear and doubt and anger. It is the time when we can begin to reach out and grow in whole new ways and in new directions. It is the time when we can begin to claim our rightful place in the world.

This process is as different for each of us as we are from each other. When we humble ourselves to reach out for the first time, we are forever changed. We can never perceive things in exactly the same way again.

A spiritual foundation is composed of all the positive things in one's life. For me it's the way I feel when I'm deeply touched by something. I look at my grandson and see him as a separate little entity, but at the same time I see his father who was so precious to me when he was little. I know it's there when someone shares their hopes and dreams with me. It sparks my soul when someone who was suffering is made well again. I'm excited and buoyed by it when I suddenly understand something which has eluded me for a long time.

I can't hold my spiritual foundation in my hand. And I don't find it in a particular place or part of the world. Nor is it borne to me by any one person. I can't give it away, but you can take it from me and I will still have plenty because it grows bigger when there is need for it. While it's always available, it's only usable when it's requested.

The Spiritual Path

I'm not talking here about religious beliefs or matters of faith and morals. I'm qualified to speak on such matters only for myself. As a matter of fact, I believe that everyone, especially women, should question whether anyone has the right to speak for them in such matters.

Over all, women and minorities have fared poorly within the confines of organized religions which, after all, have been designed and run by men. Their motives with regard to women are open to question and I believe that no honorable man would shy from such honest inspection. In the quest for our own relationship with God, we *must* question everything that we have ever been told or read or been taught in order to decide its validity for us.

I subscribe to Erich Fromm's idea that God is an infinity and that I as a finite being cannot possibly comprehend God. In fact, it seems to me that the moment I try to explain God, I have moved myself into a position in which I am trying to be God.

I feel the same way when I hear someone else trying to tell me who God is, whether it's an Indian Guru, an Episcopalian Bishop, Catholic Pope or Jewish Rabbi. I must be responsible for my own beliefs because I must walk my own path. My feeling on the issue is expressed by Gandhi who said, "Do not follow, walk beside me and be my friend." On the other hand, I would stand beside and fight for the right of all those who choose to practice their own religion. I ask only the same respect in return.

I believe that each of us must find our own way to the Power which is the source of our lives. And while I believe that other people are a wonderful source of support in this search, we're all seekers in search of ourselves. We're all looking for that part of God which is in all of us. Frequently we find it at unexpected times.

For example, I remember one woman who went with her husband to a Catholic priest for help with their failing marriage. As she described the scene, it turned into an alliance between the two men against her. They spent a lot of time talking about her *duties* and her husband's *needs*. She came away from the encounter feeling very badly about herself and trapped by the authority the two men had represented.

As she talked to me about the experience, she began to see that the two men had acted in a manner completely acceptable to both the Church and their worldly masculine identification. They had not, however, even once considered my friend's needs or wishes. In the end, she'd been bullied into submission and encouraged to see herself as selfish and self-centered.

The more she thought about the episode, the more my friend realized the God she believed in wouldn't sacrifice one person to the needs of another. She knew that she

was as important as anyone else and that she'd been looking for the wrong kind of help from two men who could
only see things through their own eyes. Their socialization
told them what they were telling her was true. They
believed they spoke with honor. But my friend was learning to trust her own honor and think for herself.

Eventually she got a divorce from her husband. When it
came, it was with a sense that what she was doing was all
right . . . and so was she.

Through this experience, my friend started on a spiritual path in pursuit of herself and her God. She came to
understand it's a journey we all need to take if we are to
reach wholeness. Although our way twists and turns
and brings us to dead ends at times, we'll know instinctively that as long as we stay on the path, we'll never
truly lose our way.

We come to know that the bricks that form the path are
constructed of self-honesty. Our fears are the bramble
bushes that line its sides, but they cannot hurt us as long
as we stay on the road. We learn that in the end, the path
will take us through our lives . . . with joy and self-love
as our companions. To the end, these companions will
support us no matter what happens to us. We learn that
even though negative things might still continue to happen, we have changed and will not continue to handle
things in the same, self-destructive manner.

Our goal for our lives must be to become other-cen-
tered. We will not rely on other fallible and imperfect
human beings, but on an ideal of a God which is perfect
and unchangeable throughout our lives. For some of us,
that means a personal God whom we talk to as in prayer.
Others may be more comfortable with the dogma and
ritual of established religions. Many women are experi-
menting with rituals to help them be in touch with the
spirits of the universe with whom they seek communion.
There is no perfect way that is suitable to all, in my view,
but each is perfect in its way for someone.

Spiritual Foundation

What I mean by the term *spiritual foundation* is an abiding sense of what gives meaning to our lives. For some that is God; for others, it's a sense of being a part of an overall continuum of the universe; for others a feeling of an over-all force for good. Whatever it is, it's essential to maintaining a positive outlook, one that nurtures and sustains us through the difficult times of our lives.

The Special Needs Of Women

Until recently there was very little research done on the needs of women in recovery, and there's still not a lot of it around. It was generally felt that women were not very different from men with respect to alcoholism and drug dependency. Therefore, treatment program design was based on what worked for men. The recovery field is still so new with respect to co-dependency that research is only just beginning.

Humane Treatment

A few years ago many detoxification centers didn't even maintain special beds for women or provide for their emotional needs. One woman I know was accepted for treatment by a detoxification center and because they didn't have her size in nightclothes, she was given a pair of men's boxer shorts and a T-shirt to wear. It was an embarrassing and dehumanizing experience for her.

Today there are still too few beds for women and, except for the high-priced places, little thought or attention is given to the amenities that would assist women in treatment. The message that comes out of this is that women are simply not valued enough to be cared for appropriately.

Child Care

There are very few facilities that allow children to stay with their recovering mothers after detoxification when her recovery and their sense of security would thrive from contact. Insurance companies prevent this from happening by levying much higher costs to the would-be provider. State and local bureaucracies prevent other agencies from entering the field by setting licensing requirements impossibly high.

Women who work to support themselves and their children are given little or no assistance in the way of child-care facilities or subsidies. They struggle to accomplish everything on a catch-as-catch-can basis. This is just one more way in which women are controlled. So, unfortunately, are their children. It seems like a very strange set of circumstances in a country that professes to have such love for its children. It sounds suspiciously like that old double standard.

Equivalent Standards

When it comes to designing treatment programs for women, the old double standard has a few extra wrinkles. This is where we see triple and quadruple stigmas added to the cloud of prejudice that has always been over women. There is the double stigma of being a woman first of all and secondly of being a woman who is alcoholic or drug-addicted. The triple stigma is attached to women who are members of racial minorities or are lesbians or bisexual and are also chemically dependent. Finally we see the quadruple stigma against women who are lesbians or bisexuals, are members of a racial minority and are addicts.

Men suffer discrimination if they are actively alcoholic or members of minorities too. The difference is that society holds out many more opportunities for them to receive help with their addictions. Check the services available in any state. Those that are strictly for men greatly outnumber those for women. And when men leave treatment to re-establish themselves again, they make more money than women can by almost half. They rarely, if ever, find it necessary to go on welfare so they can take care of their children. The training and educational opportunities available to them far outnumber those for women. People still have trouble relating to women as the breadwinners for their families.

Freedom From Fear

One of the greatest fears women have is that their children will be taken away from them for good if they go for treatment of alcoholism or drug dependence or admit that they are in trouble emotionally. But we don't help women handle this concern in a way that would make both them and their children feel they were getting what they need.

Instead there are enormous barriers in the form of government regulations which effectively deter agencies, nonprofit or otherwise, from adding child care to their recovery programs. This is one of the powerful reasons why there are so few programs in the United States which allow for children and their mothers to stay together during treatment.

Only recently has there been any real discussion about creating a national child care program that takes honest notice of the fact that the majority of women who are mothers and work outside the home do so because of need.

Child abuse is on the rise, not declining. This includes incidents from unthinking abuse that happens in everyday life such as verbal harassment, to beating children to death. Sexual abuse is also either on the increase or being reported more now that women are refusing to be victims any longer and are finding ways to help themselves and each other.

It seems to me there is another kind of double standard. We applaud and revere motherhood, but we forget that human beings, not robots, are mothers. Then, when there is a breach of the standards that society sets for mothers, we're shocked and all too ready to blame the woman who is the victim of our own unrealistic and frequently outdated expectations.

Delores' Story

Typical of some of the kinds of damage that can be done to families who find themselves in need of help from society is the case of Delores:

> When she finally admitted that she needed help, Delores was at the end of her resources. An alcoholic and a drug addict, she was on welfare with her four children. Her husband had left her two years earlier because of his own addiction. At her initial interview at the treatment center where she went for help, she admitted she was also bulimic.
>
> Delores' two sisters, who'd been supportive early on in her illness, had finally given up hope for her. They concentrated their efforts instead on trying to save her children. While they meant well, neither sister could take in all four of the children while Delores recuperated. Delores definitely did not want her children separated and she didn't want them to stay with her parents. Her father had abused her sexually when she was a child and she wouldn't allow him free access to her children. The only alternative was a foster home where the children could be placed near their mother's treatment center. Understandably the children didn't want to leave their own home, but Delores assured them it was the only way to help them all get back on their feet again.
>
> Delores did well in her treatment center. She worked hard to understand her addiction and saw her children every chance she could get. While still in the center, she got a job and started saving money while making plans to take her children back. Delores envisioned them all living in a decent house in a safe neighborhood. There she could once again take over her responsibilities and work toward getting off welfare.
>
> As an 11th-grade graduate, Delores was not skilled in anything more than the typing she had learned earlier in a government-sponsored training program. However, she was bright and quick to learn and was willing to work hard. No matter how hard she worked though, she couldn't earn enough money to support herself and her four children without assistance.
>
> When it came time for Delores to leave the center, she still hadn't been able to find appropriate housing for her

family. She had no choice but to leave them in the foster home while she moved in temporarily with a couple of women with whom she'd been in treatment. Still Delores felt hopeful. She was working at a decent job, earning enough money to take care of her children with the assistance of food stamps, a public housing certificate and Medicare for their health needs. Delores felt she was at last offering a positive role model to her children and that the future held the promise that they might one day all be free of the welfare system.

It took another six months before a large enough apartment was found to accommodate Delores' family. When she went to the housing office to sign the necessary papers, however, the clerk handling it informed Delores that she earned $100 a month too much to qualify for assistance. She said Delores would have to quit her job and go back on welfare or lose the apartment. Devastated is too mild a word for what Delores felt. At $13,500.00 a year, there was no possible way she could support her family. She would have to take her children back into the dead-end lifestyle she thought she'd been working her way out of. Because she couldn't stand being separated from her children any longer, she agreed to quit her job and move into the new apartment.

While it was big enough, the apartment was not in a very good neighborhood. The first thing that happened was that her oldest daughter's bike, her most prized possession, was stolen from in front of their house.

As they settled into the neighborhood, it became apparent to Delores that neighbors were dealing drugs to people from outside the area. Her children came home more often than not angry and fearful because of arguments with the other children. Like Delores' children, they too had very little and were constantly fighting against a world they felt was hostile and in which they felt powerless.

Delores was not feeling a whole lot better than the children. She did everything she could to create a comforting and pleasant home life, but the outside world kept pushing its way into her home.

After she'd been in the apartment for a year, Delores discovered that all four of her daughters had been sexually abused by a man who'd come into her life as a friend. He'd seemed a wonderful gift to her and her children, taking them places and being there for them all in a very loving and respectful way. He even babysat for the girls while Delores went shopping. All of her friends thought she was very fortunate to find a man who seemed such a perfect companion and seemed to need so little in return from them.

Perhaps the worst part of Delores' whole story is that her daughters were beginning to lose faith in her. They saw her struggling to care for them, but they didn't see their lives getting any better. They were beginning to look outside for some relief from their lives.

Society failed Delores and her children. Their lives are in a downward spiral and her daughters in turn will probably be caught up in the welfare system, which is not designed to work with individuals. How much more sense it makes for society to provide sensible and supportive assistance to women in need of treatment *and* their children before they lose themselves and each other.

A Support System

Women who are co-dependent spend a lot of their lives trying to live up to what they think other people think of them. That means they must be constantly aware of how others *seem* to feel or think. They must guess what others want from them. As we have seen earlier, this tendency is used against women in their formative years. Recovery requires the assistance of people who are aware of this tendency and can help these women achieve and maintain a solid reality base. Unconditional acceptance and clear feedback are two of the tools needed to form this foundation.

It's important to have trustworthy people in the support system of co-dependent women. These support people must be well enough acquainted with them to know when they're lapsing into the kind of half magical/half fantasy thinking that leads them to put their hopes in the wrong people, places or things. These people must be capable of honest, clear feedback in appropriate fashion. Mutual respect is an important ingredient in these relationships.

Time To Recover

Women have so many different needs . . . physical, emotional and spiritual. Like their alcoholic sisters, co-dependent women need a lot of time for recovery, and they, too, need safety while in the process.

If I could snap my fingers and magically give both groups just one gift, it would be time. Time to rest, time to spend with positive support systems, time to learn to care for themselves and time to learn about what has happened to them so they can make plans to move forward.

Traditionally women have very little time to call their own. Most of it seems to belong to someone or something else. The demands on the average woman are such that she can rarely justify seeing to her own needs if anyone around her has unmet needs also. If she puts off the wants of others in order to see to her own needs, she's called selfish.

Education

If I had a second wish for women, it would be for education to help them understand the true nature of their disease. Then they could begin to know they're not at fault. I'd like them to learn they *are* worthwhile people and that there is a way up out of the trap in which they find themselves. This education should also be available to the world so it, too, can dispose of centuries of stereotyping women. The results would be positive for both men and women since to keep one group down is ultimately to hold both back.

Self-Esteem

My third wish would come naturally out of the growth to be gained from the first two: that women learn to love and value themselves for no other reason than that they exist.

Women who are victimized by abuse can't possibly love themselves while still caught in such traps. Healthy people who care about themselves don't permit that kind of abuse. They wouldn't tolerate it from others and certainly treat themselves with more kindness.

One of the worst burdens co-dependents carry is low self-esteem, exacerbated by isolation from people who can give them unconditional accepting love and support. That's one of the reasons why I don't think there's a better choice than self-help groups in which to begin recovery. There co-dependents meet others like themselves who've been wrung out and hung up to dry by the world. In these groups they learn there is nothing fundamentally wrong with them and if they don't like the lives they've constructed, they have the opportunity to change them for the better. When changed attitudes are followed by positive action, whole new lives can be built out of the ashes of the old ones.

CHAPTER 8

Barriers
To Change

Resistance To Change

There are so many barriers to recovery for people coming to grips with co-dependence and addiction. Their internalized resistance to change is probably the most powerful of these barriers and this resistance is something that only the individual can make a decision to give up.

Recovery can only happen in direct proportion to the changes that occur within us.

It's only when *we allow* our attitudes to change, that our lives can change.

When we come to understand what things are really basic to our beliefs about ourselves, our relationship to that self and to the rest of the world must change. Resistance can't remain in a truly open mind. To illustrate what happens when new information enters the mind, when I add a word to what I have already written on my comput-er, all the words after it move automatically to accommo-date the new spaces occupied. The minds of normally functioning people are like that. They are capable of infi-nite additions and adjustments in their brains. This is not to say that their behavior is necessarily altered, but it can never again be unaffected by new information. However, refusal to change one's behavior in spite of newfound knowledge that the old way is no longer appropriate is really gross resistance.

Unfortunately, we see this resistance all the time in people who are too afraid of what changed behavior will bring. This kind of fear is not an excuse, it's just a moti-vation. Like fear, we can change what we choose to be motivated by in our lives.

Helen's Story

The following illustration is about a woman we'll call Helen who suddenly came face to face with herself and her negativity and the need to change her behavior.

As late as my 30s, I was willing to believe almost anything negative about myself. That's why I was so open to being devalued by others. I wasn't able to see that such attacks said far more about the people making them than they did about me. I didn't know that I could stop being so passive, and I didn't know how to respond in any other way. I didn't even know that I need not respond at all if I didn't want to, no matter how much others wanted me to do so.

From the way I'd been brought up, I inferred that I wasn't good enough, I wasn't smart enough, I wasn't really worth as much as my siblings. It's clear to me today that my parents didn't tell me these things. It was my interpretation of my observations that made them seem true to me.

It was a wonderful revelation, akin to a spiritual awakening, when I came to understand I could change my personality, I could rebuild my character according to my own desires. I could heal old wounds by opening them up to the healing of self-honesty and forgiveness for myself and others. I could see from that moment on I could be conscious of my choices and, in the process, recreate myself in *my* true image . . . not someone else's. In essence, I could take back my own power.

What this woman experienced is the same painful process addicted people go through in the course of their individual diseases. It isn't hard to see the similarities, and it's even possible to see that the need to control the people, places and things in the co-dependent's life might be rooted in the same kind of fear of losing control addicts suffer from also.

In my work over the past 14 years with alcoholic and/ or drug-addicted women who were also co-dependent, I've found that most of them, certainly all who were children of alcoholics, fit this pattern. All are dependent people with some of their dependencies more obvious than others, at least to onlookers. They themselves are very unwilling to admit that they are at all dependent.

Forming Bad Relationships

Nonrecovered co-dependent women are frequently unable to pair with people who are healthy individuals capable of forming good relationships. Yet they're so insecure and so fearful to be alone they seem to go far out of their way to become involved in relationships . . . any relationship . . . to avoid being alone.

Because these women are involved at an unconscious level in efforts to work out their primary relationships, it's inevitable that they'll keep on finding those people who most remind them of their mothers or fathers, or whomever the person was who constituted this primary relationship.

When a family includes one or more alcoholic parents, the children are in some manner victimized by co-dependence.

Take the following familiar example: A child who doesn't bring friends home for fear that she'll be embarrassed by her actively alcoholic parent. Such a child has learned that home is not a supportive place. She knows the alcoholic is not to be trusted, nor can she trust the nondrinking parent who's proven she or he cannot handle the drinker.

This child's co-dependency could show up later as an unwillingness to trust *anyone*. As a result, she may be capable only of surface involvement in relationships, or be tremendously possessive of the people in her life. She might also be possessive of the things she owns, being unwilling to share them or to be capable of generosity because she fears she'll end up not having enough for herself. Such people might have a great need to know just exactly what those around them are doing at all times, exerting as much control as possible over them. And they would probably work very hard to maintain an impenetrable facade around their home lives.

Others might continually see their hopes and plans destroyed because the money that would've provided for them was spent on alcohol or drugs or gambling, or any other number of addictions or obsessions. These people could feel they could only form attachments with people just like the addictive parent. At least then they would know what to expect from them.

An example of the power of co-dependence in a family system is the case where the alcoholic parent (or parents) stop drinking, but the family relationships stay more or less the same. Such a family could still be in denial that there was ever anything wrong except for the drinking. This could just be a great way to continue to scape-goat the alcoholic. Or it could reflect the fact that life had certainly improved for the family with the cessation of drinking. What is true, however, is that fear, doubt and insecurity raise their ugly heads when a co-dependent family structure is threatened by change of any kind.

Change comes hard to people who aren't in touch with their resources or who feel they've begun with too few.

To be willing to change the context in which they live their lives requires a leap of faith not many people are able to make, unless they feel supported and guided through it. However, being able to accept the support and guidance available requires a degree of trust that recovering co-dependents are not able to give easily. Having had only negatives in which to place their trust in the past, they've come to believe that trusting anyone or anything is a bad thing to do.

It's just this kind of spiraling thinking that works against recovery. Risk has meant failure. Therefore, risk seems useless. Failure has meant a loss of self-esteem. Therefore risking failure is too costly. Resources are severely limited, therefore almost anything is too costly. Better to remain quiet and in the background, rather than lose anymore. Or to grab for everything available in preparation for the time when nothing is forthcoming.

What happens sometimes to people who have few resources and are afraid to risk them is that they fail to develop as individuals and as people. They continue to rely on the same answers to life's problems, achieving the same kinds of results. For some, this means that generation after generation are affected. For example, people who fall on hard times, must accept welfare support and are unable to stop accepting it. Too frequently their children wind up making many of the same mistakes and they themselves fall into the welfare trap.

Children of addiction have too few resources. They're unable to develop emotionally. They look in all the wrong places for support and information. They pass on from generation to generation their inability to make life work.

A good example of this kind of dysfunction is the family with one or more alcoholic parents who were actively drinking during the children's early years. These children learn to function in the context of dysfunction. Children may copy the parental example by drinking in alcoholic fashion and by stopping their drinking . . . as did their parents. Then the family relationship will shift from being based on alcoholic to sober behavior . . . although it's still based on dysfunction.

Recovery looks very different from mere sober behavior. In recovery, all kinds of changes must take place in the family relationships when the individuals change themselves.

The Enemies Within

There are many well-entrenched enemies of recovery which must be overcome before any real progress can be made. We have to face them, call them by name and admit they are a part of us. They are the shortcomings that keep us strangers to ourselves and work against the self-love that is essential to growth and happiness. Often people panic at the thought of the changes they must make, not realizing that time is on their side as long as they're working toward recovery.

Denial

Like fear, denial may seem to serve a useful purpose in the defense of our physical and emotional well-being. The problem is that neither serves us very well spiritually. As we come to learn, we must serve our spiritual needs first if we are to recover in a meaningful long-lasting way.

Denial is self-deceit, even though when we use it, our conscious intention may be to fool others. To deny a thing is so is actually an attempt to control the people, places and things around us. When we do that, we are constructing a world of our own, one in which others cannot join us as we are, only as we wish them to be.

The other side of the coin is that trying to control everything around us is a full-time job. Therefore, we are the most controlled of all. Think about the absurdity of trying to control others by living up to their expectations of us. We're stuck with trying to live up to what we think we think of us.

The purpose of all this deceit is the satisfaction of our own self-centered wishes. When we're self-centered, we can't be *other*-centered. There is, then, no way we can be spiritually centered when we are in denial. As a result, we end up isolated and alone, unable to break out of our self-constructed and self-imposed prisons without help.

Isolation

It's precisely this isolation that presents the greatest impediment to recovery from chemical dependence, from co-dependence or any dependence-based disease. Think of the child suffering abuse at home. The most fearful thing the perpetrator can think of is that the child will tell someone. Whole populations have been controlled by fear and isolation imposed by dictators to keep their people in line. Families are shut off from friends by the admonition, "Whatever happens within these four walls, stays within these four walls."

Whenever new ideas are introduced into a society, life can never be the same again. That's why totalitarian governments try so hard to keep their people isolated. Lies have a harder time flourishing in an open and participatory citizen government. The same principle is at work all the way down through society's strata, including one-to-one relationships.

It wasn't so long ago that women, for instance, were denied the right to an education . . . beyond training in those skills which would enhance her worth in the home. Job opportunities were so limited that unmarried women could not earn a decent living. Today, even though women have undoubtedly come a long way, they must still fight harder than men for their right to advance according to their abilities and willingness to work hard.

Lifetime Of Work

Denial is so thoroughly ingrained in our way of life as co-dependents and dependent people that it takes a very long time to see it in all of its forms. I don't think it's possible for co-dependent people to see all of the manifestations of their denial in a lifetime. And even if it were possible, I believe it's the easiest behavior to slip back into whenever we feel threatened because it's been used as a survival tool, protecting us from shame and the pain of rejection. It defends our negative, false pride that says, "I dare not let anyone see me as I am because they will judge me harshly and find me unacceptable."

One of the worst things that can happen to co-dependent people is to be rejected. Depending upon the degree of self-worth they possess, any situation and any person can be a potential source of rejection.

Randy's Story

To illustrate, let's look at this example.

I'd been driving the school bus for three years. My whole identity was wrapped up in how well I did it. I worried about things like . . . Did the children like me? Did they like the way I drove? Did their parents trust my driving? Was I the best of all the drivers?

If for some reason one of the children was upset with me, I worried all night until the next morning to see if he or she was over it. If so, I would feel better until the next time.

The worst part of all that suffering was I knew how abnormally I was reacting but I couldn't help myself. I couldn't share my feelings with anyone because I knew they'd think I was crazy. I certainly was not the picture of emotional health.

Randy is a true co-dependent personality. The bus driving job was made to order because she was in a position of authority or leadership. The children were captive in the bus until they reached their homes. Because she was the only grownup on the bus, they had to interact with her. In short, they needed her. Her self-esteem had reached such a low point, she needed them, too, because adults were too fearful for her to face at that time.

By taking the bus-driving job, Randy could act as if everything was all right in her life. Her denial of the truth was undetectable to others. But she couldn't remain stationary at that emotional level because her isolation was too debilitating. She was also drinking too much, making the facade of wellness fairly brittle and more difficult to maintain.

Fear

Just as denial has the power to isolate, so does fear. The co-dependent who's never experienced the empowerment of unconditional love or freedom from want can't be comfortable in her own skin. The world is a dangerous place for such an individual.

It seems impossible to think of being completely without fear and it probably is for all practical purposes. If a truck is heading toward me, for instance, and I am in its way, I will certainly have a reaction which is rooted in my will to survive. This kind of fear could be described as a healthy fear.

Other kinds of fear are not as easily explained or accommodated. The fear of change is coupled with the human need for security. Too many changes made too quickly in anyone's life can cause more stress than someone can handle. We need to know where our boundaries are, where we can be safe and to whom we matter.

If we lose loved ones in close succession or our livelihood is insecure or we're unable to feel at home in our living space, our survival instinct is threatened. If we don't have a spiritual foundation for our lives, we'll probably suffer greatly when catastrophe occurs.

It's vital to learn when our own behavior is such that we continually create problems for ourselves. If we think other people are responsible for all of our problems, there's no way out. We'll always create more trouble for ourselves while blaming others for it. The payoff in this pattern of behavior is that we can always claim that our troubles are not our fault, that we're just hapless victims of circumstances.

The Payoff For Not Changing

While it may seem strange to use the word *payoff* in this context, there's always a payoff for any behavior. Rational human beings always do things in order to create an effect. When our behavior is thought out in advance and our motivation is clearly positive, chances are the payoff (or the outcome) will be positive. When our behavior is calculated, consciously or unconsciously, to benefit only ourselves, then our motivation and our payoff will be completely selfish. Selfish motivation is usually created in secret and tends to isolate those practicing it.

Maryanne's Story

We see this behavior in the following instance.

When my husband graduated from college and took his first job, we thought we were really rich. We'd got along on so little while he was going through school that his salary seemed enormous to us.

In spite of the fact that I'd never really handled money or budgets, I took over the running of the household, including paying the bills and maintaining our budget. I felt my husband worked hard enough and that the home should be my job entirely. He seemed happy to be relieved of those responsibilities and never asked if I was having any trouble with it.

What neither of us took into account at the time was that I'd been brought up in a home where money was very scarce until I was a teenager. Then my father was hired by a company that paid him extremely well. After that, there didn't seem to be any limit to the money I had to spend.

I had absolutely no idea how to manage money or a household, for that matter. Money really scared me to death. But like the perfect adult daughter and co-dependent I am, I was determined not to let anyone know I didn't know something that I thought I *should* know. As a matter of fact, I was always *shoulding* on myself about something or other.

Of course, my ignorance of the mechanics of money management being what it was, it wasn't long before I had us over our heads with monthly payments and the like. The worst part was that I kept it all to myself because I couldn't face being seen as a failure.

Although it seems unbelievable to me now, I started digging a really deep hole for myself by writing out the checks for the bills at the end of the month, putting them into envelopes, even stamping them and then putting several of them back into a drawer without mailing them. I then went on and spent the money from our salary again to meet daily expenses.

When I think about it now, I can't imagine how I managed the balancing act I undertook. The dunning letters and telephone calls began coming before long and I went on constant alert to intercept them before my husband got them. When things got too bad for me to hold together any more, I called my husband's mother and borrowed money from her, confessing what I'd done and asking her not to tell her son.

Finally, my husband found out about some of what I'd done, although his mother never did tell him about what she'd given me. He took over the checkbook and I never handled it again. My husband was also a good co- dependent. He, like me, belonged to the 'all or nothing school of adult childhood.' We alternated back and forth on being the hero or heroine in our little homespun dramas. We never worked together to solve anything.

As a good co-dependent, Maryanne was playing the heroine at home, without having the means to maintain her part. Her fear of insecurity and need to be indispensable in some way to her husband moved her toward self-destruction, taking everyone who'd been willing to be involved in her manipulation along with her.

The truth is Maryanne couldn't have done the things she did without the tacit consent of people like her husband and her mother-in-law. Her husband clearly looked the other way while their money was mismanaged. His mother had been willing to deceive him about the money she was loaning to Maryanne. It's possible his mother thought her son really knew about the loan and had put Maryanne up to getting the loan without seeming to involve him. Whatever was happening, everyone involved was following his or her own agenda, while going on as if nothing unusual was happening.

That kind of co-dependent behavior can go on forever while the participants change nothing but the surface difficulties. Underneath it's business as usual in order to keep all the players in the game . . . although their roles constantly shift and change.

I use the word *game* advisedly, even though I'm aware how hateful it is to be co-dependent. But I believe it's a descriptive word for what is happening. There are winners and losers in the co-dependent game of life. There are rules and prizes. And while each game has a beginning and an end, the match may go on for a lifetime fueled by the fear of what will happen if it's ever finished.

Negativity

One of the greatest barriers to recovery is constructed over the years, stone by stone, as we substitute negative for positive thinking. The process is so slow and seems so rational that we deny it happened at all. What it leads to is an almost impenetrable wall of self-doubt and lack of self-esteem.

Over and over, any kind of positive thought, any hopeful sign for the future, any possibility that things will change for the better, is greeted with skepticism. In part these conclusions are ingrained from childhood, conditioned by disappointments that are blown up bigger than life. Eventually negativity becomes a powerful coping mechanism.

Just as importantly, negativity can also be used as a weapon. I would guess almost everyone knows someone who fights against recovery through responding negatively to any and all efforts to help. While I believe all co-dependent people do so to some degree, there are people who seem to have a vested interest in refusing to recover. For these people, fear is one of the overwhelming forces that motivates against change. But it's important not to overlook the tremendous effect their egos play in fighting change. Most often co-dependents speak of their inability to trust anyone, but what they really mean is that they're *unwilling* to do so. To them, choosing to place their confidence in another means making a value judgment about who'll be the recipient of that trust. In their minds, however, there's no one who has enough integrity or honesty to be relied upon for anything important.

There's also a great deal of anger and unwillingness to forgive others for what co-dependents see as transgressions against them in the past. The truth is they frequently choose people in whom to place their faith who couldn't possibly live up to their expectations.

One woman I know, for example, is scrupulously faithful in her attendance at ACoA and AA meetings. She has never, in all the four years she's been attending meetings, asked anyone to be her sponsor in either group. When questioned about it, she says, "I know I should, but . . .".

As a result, her progress in recovery has been painfully slow, full of relapses and puzzling to anyone without the background to understand it. This woman spends most of her time alone, refusing to share her feelings or ask for help. Her old friends Justification and Rationalization keep her walled up in her self-centered world where she manages to avoid spiritual growth almost entirely. Attempts to talk to her about the issue are met with anger and rebellion.

Another woman, also faithful in her attendance, has asked many people to be her sponsor but always for the wrong reasons. When they fail her, as she knew they would when she chose them, she uses the loss as an opportunity to justify what she calls her "inability" to trust. Confronted with her behavior, she denies that she deliberately chose someone whose normal conduct falls far short of the traits she supposedly desires.

Why pick such a sponsor in the first place? To fulfill the prophecy that no one is to be trusted.

Relationships With Other Co-dependents

If it's hard for individual co-dependents to resolve their issues and move through recovery, the difficulties of two or more people locked together in dysfunction are multiplied.

Their relationships are founded in negativity and may include issues of anger and fear, coupled with pride and self-centeredness both individually and through the third entity formed when they join their lives together. It's a fundamental law of nature that the whole can be greater than the sum of its parts. One and one can make three when it's people being added. Not only must the members of such a relationship protect themselves, they must protect the relationship against all possible encroachments.

These are the people we see attending recovery meetings together at all times because they must know what the other is doing or saying. If either or both ask anyone to be a sponsor, they agree in advance it won't be anyone who could put any distance between them. Sometimes they'll even ask the members of another couple to sponsor them individually. They know at some level such an arrangement only encourages their enmeshment.

Mary's And George's Story

As an example I offer Mary and George, both in their late 20s and both addicts, in addition to coming from untreated co-dependent alcoholic homes. When they met, it was like seeing their image in a mirror. Unfortunately, like a mirror image, they didn't go beneath surface similarities in their assessments of each other. They jumped to all kinds of conclusions and saw themselves as being completely compatible. They felt their strengths complemented each other perfectly and were married almost immediately.

Given the facts stacked against them, these two very quickly descended through the milestones of their addiction, ending up together in a shelter for homeless people. From there they were sent to a detoxification center by the police.

From detox Mary was persuaded to go into long-term treatment at a coed halfway house in another state. George, on the other hand, refused further help and returned to the shelter.

Mary did well at first. She was young and her body and mind mended well after she was withdrawn from the drugs. For the first time in a long time she was sleeping and eating properly.

George worried her though. She thought about him almost constantly. He didn't know where she was because he'd hit the streets when Mary had been taken to the detox center. Finally, when Mary began to feel well, she managed to contact him to let him know where she was staying. Mary believed she could help George benefit from recovery just as she had. What she didn't know was that for either of them to recover meant the almost certain end of their relationship and their marriage.

With that initial contact there began a series of pushing and pulling maneuvers between them in their efforts to regain control. Mary pushed George to enter treatment and George kept trying to pull Mary out of it.

George couldn't tolerate that anyone else might have influence over Mary. He felt she was his perfect mate and couldn't bear to lose her. He also believed no one could love her or care for her the way he did. The staff at the treatment center represented a great threat to him. On the other hand, Mary could not bear to continue to act independent of George in recovery: She felt that she must have him with her for her to succeed.

Mary finally left treatment and returned with George to shelter living. But by that time she'd experienced enough in treatment so that her disease had been altered and she no longer thought the same way that George did about everything. She stayed with George for some time, but she could no longer tolerate not having goals, living in deprivation or feeling less worthwhile than others. The greatest miracle was that she continued to attend AA meetings and didn't drink or take drugs. George refused to join her in her self-help groups and he refused to go for counseling. Most divisive of all, he continued to drink.

Ironically, it was George's drinking, the thing that had
first brought them together, that was increasingly more
difficult for Mary to manage living with daily. The longer
she was sober, the more she noticed things: how badly he
smelled when he came home, how boring his conversation
was when he was drunk. She resented the money he
spent on alcohol. Worst of all, Mary was beginning to feel
ashamed of George. She hated herself for all these feelings. She felt disloyal to him. She wanted the feelings of
love that they had shared back. Her heart was breaking.
Yet she could not and would not choose to return to the
way she had lived with him. She had truly experienced a
spiritual awakening and knew that she never wanted to
lose the vision of a better life that sobriety promised.

Before long Mary looked for and took a job as a
saleswoman at, interestingly enough, a women's credit
union. The part of Mary that wanted something better for
herself was reaching out to other women who were role
models for the kind of person she wished to be.

During this time, George felt Mary slipping away from
him. He did everything he could think of (barring violence
which he knew she wouldn't tolerate) to convince Mary to
return to her old ways. Unfortunately, he never seriously
considered changing his ways to more closely match Mary's.
Inevitably they split up, more because the bonds of their
co-dependency were loosened by Mary's change in
thinking than because of anything else.

George and Mary are good examples of what can
happen when two card-carrying co-dependents come together. They're role models in whom we can see the
shortcomings we may share with them.

They believed, for instance, that they needed each other; that they were meant for each other; that they had to
be together in everything. The truth is that what they
called need was the stranglehold they had on each other.
The belief that they were meant for each other was simply
their instinctive recognition that each of them was willing
to grab on and hold tightly to the other. They filled each

other's desperate out-of-balance need for emotional security. The idea that they had to be together was fear saying, "Don't let him/her out of my sight for a minute or something might change and I'll lose control and be alone again." There's no possibility for growth in a pairing like this. Growth is a terrible threat to the co-dependent's misguided instincts for self-preservation.

Fortunately the ability to grow and change is fundamental to the nature of human beings. That's why Mary was able to break out of the relationship that was choking off her life.

It's impossible to predict whether Mary and George would ultimately have stayed together if both had entered treatment. We know the odds against remaining together were great when only one was in recovery. We also know that, because of her dependence on alcohol, Mary reached a point at which public intervention was necessary, when she was taken to detox by police. It was from that serendipitous event that Mary made the move to recovery for herself.

George had also been taken to the detox center, but he was unwilling to remain in treatment. He allowed his dependence on alcohol and the false pride that said he could handle his own affairs blind him to the truth about his condition. He was very ill and had lost the ability to act in his own best interests.

Frequently in familial relationships the members are as tightly bound as people like George and Mary. Literature is full of examples of parents binding their children to them through an overwhelming sense of guilt, responsibility, shame, fear or sometimes greed. Whole cultures have been based on this kind of binding, but we call it "tradition," and we have a whole set of laws designed to punish anyone who tries to step outside of the norm.

Dictatorships and totalitarian governments operate completely on the co-dependent idea that the people need the State, and of course, the dictator needs the people to keep him in power. The most dangerous threat to this form of government, therefore, is the same as it was for George, that members in the partnership would begin to think for themselves instead of following blindly along the path of self-imprisonment.

No matter how much we try to deny it, we blaze our own paths to self-destruction. We're responsible for the quality of our own lives. No matter how much we may want to blame others, we're responsible for much of the pain we have suffered. Life itself is a process from birth to death. Recovery is a part of that process. It must be lived through a day at a time with as open a mind as we can manage if we're to understand our role.

CHAPTER 9

Working Through Our Barriers

Recognizing Denial

In order to work through denial women must first be able to recognize it. To do that, we must be willing to take risks. We must be willing to face ourselves squarely and take responsibility for the consequences of our actions. We need positive role models and people in our lives who can support us through the process.

Alcoholics Anonymous was started in 1935. Many other special interest groups have sprung up since that first one, all recognizing the importance of banding together to help their members recover from the soul sickness that overdependence on people, places and things can cause.

All of these groups have as a basic goal helping the sufferers *first to come to grips with their denial about the nature of their own illness*, whatever it may be. Then, they must be willing to *embrace self-honesty* in the pursuit of a spiritual foundation for a new way of life. Self-honesty is basic to all the steps the individual must take on the road to recovery. We *maintain progress* through daily attention to our responses to the ordinary details of living and, by continued *sharing* of our *progress* with at least one other person whom we have made the decision to trust. That person may be a member of the recovery group or a therapist who understands the nature of co-dependence.

Learning To Trust

Learning to trust is essential to recovery from all dependence-based diseases. It's the one commodity the co-dependent felt she could least afford when growing up. From her perspective, trust was almost always misplaced or there wasn't anyone available who could be considered trustworthy. Since unhappiness usually followed her efforts to move out of isolation and toward people, she probably feels that she can't even trust herself to make correct choices.

In recovery it's often necessary to make an intellectual decision to trust someone else. That's not a risk taken easily but it's a risk that's essential to recovery.

Once the decision to trust has been made, it frequently seems as if the whole world opens up to the recoverer. So much seems to make sense and fall into place. So many things that were formerly too hard to comprehend now seem simple. Old fears disappear as if by magic. It's an amazing thing to watch the world suddenly make sense to someone who had thought it never would. When someone makes a decision to trust someone else, that person has also made a decision to come out of isolation and join other people in living.

Facing Ourselves

It's easy to see when a person in recovery refuses to take the suggestions given. Argument takes the place of willingness and isolation remains a constant in the person's life. It's clear that if no one else can cross the protective wall around the newcomer, then the person who built it and maintains it can't get out of it either. It's a self-constructed prison. That person will continue to look for others to blame for her predicament, refusing to look within. There's an unconscious choice to remain stuck in negative thinking, spurning any evidence to the contrary that new choices can be made.

How much better it is to face ourselves squarely, to learn to see and accept ourselves with love and compassion. It's in this way we can begin to change the ground rules by which we've lived so unsuccessfully.

Changing Our Framework

One of the ways in which we can change the context or framework of our lives is to begin to focus on positives instead of negatives.

Growing up as co-dependents we had no balancing view of ourselves. Our shortcomings were pointed out to us, but rarely our good points. We came to believe that our shortcomings defined us, not realizing that they simply stood for the distance between us and what we thought of as perfection. They weren't in themselves proof of our inadequacy. On the contrary, our shortcomings really point to the multi-faceted sides of our personalities. No one is just one-dimensional.

We're all capable of more than one kind of reaction to similar situations. Much will depend on how we feel at the time, how aware we are of ourselves and what we wish to accomplish, and even who it is we're interacting with. We've all known (and may have been) street angels/house devils. These are the people who care a lot more about how the people outside their homes feel about them than the people inside their homes, so they're completely different in both places.

To give a really extreme example, I recently saw some home movies of Adolf Hitler talking pleasantly and lovingly to children. This was the same man who ordered the death of millions of children just because he did not like Jews. Even a monster like that could be capable of dual responses given his feelings at the moment. Why should we expect ourselves to be absolutely controlled and unchanging in all situations?

On the contrary, if we're judgmental sometimes, we can be compassionate at other times. If we're sometimes stingy, we can also be generous.

Our actions are based upon choice. We can choose to be positive or negative in a given situation. We can choose to be aware of our responses and we can then choose to make them positive ones. By making these choices as much as possible, we change the context of our lives. While it's the hardest thing in the world for a person who has assumed negativity to do, the principle of changing negatives to positives is a very simple one. But it must be practiced daily. The good news is, just as negativity had become the context in which life was lived, being positive will also become a way of life. If this all sounds a little Pollyanna-ish, don't let that stop you from trying it.

Growing Up

Young people normally move toward maturity by flipping back and forth between different behaviors, trying them out, testing their limits, and building character. In recovery we go through the same process, not for the second time, but for the first, as we build our own character and formulate a basis for living founded in maturity. Finally we function far more often in a positive, independent and interdependent fashion.

We can't reach perfection, of course, much less stay there. To believe that is to deny our basic fallibility as human beings. What we can do is come to know and be kinder to ourselves. We can notice ourselves as growing entities and can value ourselves for our willingness to change no matter how much pain that may cause at times.

Unfortunately, pain seems to be a prerequisite to change in any aspect of our personalities. The doors of the mind creak open ever so slowly and light enters only weakly at first. Progress is achieved grudgingly, no matter how many times we experience the positive effects of making the changes that are in our own best interests. If we make the pursuit of positive aspects of our personalities a goal in itself, our attitudes will change about ourselves as well as others.

Once we've changed our attitudes, like the words on the computer screen, nothing else is exactly the same as it was. This factor is the whole basis for continued growth throughout our lives.

CHAPTER 10

The Process Of Discovering More

Among the things that make one person different from another are the everyday choices we make along
the way in life. Those choices are affected by the influ-
ences around us.

Recovery from co-dependency and addiction is the process of discovering *more:*

- More life
- More ability to love one's self and others
- More insight into the way things work
- And more depth of understanding at all levels

Best of all perhaps is the newfound knowledge that
there are always more choices to be made in any given
situation than might first appear.

The very idea of being able to make such choices is an
unnerving one, for a lot of reasons. Questions such as:

"Who will I be if I make new life choices? Will I like myself; will others like me, and I them? How will I fit in?"

These are the kinds of questions which are of particular importance to women because our society still wants to give women less real power over their own lives. Because this powerlessness is so pervasive, it takes women a long time to see it in themselves as something that can be changed.

How many women go through their 20s, 30s, 40s and 50s feeling more like children than adults? How often do they continue to try to receive absolution for being themselves? How often are they unable to stand up and be counted for what they believe because they fear the disapproval of others? How often do they remain caught in a kind of time warp, having matured in every way but emotionally?

Ellen's Story

A woman we shall call Ellen is an example:

My mother had undergone an extremely serious operation and I had gone to her home to stand in as nurse, housekeeper and go-fer. But she hadn't been home from the hospital for half an hour before she began treating me like a child, giving me detailed instructions about how to do everything.

She'd always been like that with me and I with her. Not my age, my social position, nor my professional achievements had ever influenced her to treat me with the respect I felt I deserved. Nor did I demand to be treated appropriately. More often than not, I tried to appease her by acting the child. So she saw me as a child still, not capable of managing without supervision.

Her extensive perfectionism about everything was not limited to her interactions with me, of course, but I was feeling particularly burdened by it now. When I found an excuse to get out of the house for a while, I was feeling as if I wouldn't be able to manage staying the next ten days.

I struggled with myself not to be negative or judgmental about her, to hold my tongue and avoid arguments. Unfortunately, my silence was typical behavior for me when I was with her. I'd always justified not answering her sharply with some excuse: 'She's sick, I don't want to make her worse' or 'I should be able to handle her better' or 'What is the use? I'll never convince her.' The resulting frustration and resentment stayed with me until the opportunity came along to let off steam, usually inappropriately.

This time I was in recovery from the co-dependence that had kept me immobilized and bitter as far back as I could remember. I hadn't stayed in my mother's house for this long since I left it many years earlier, at the age of 18, to be married. Today I know my marriage was just an escape, a way to change one co-dependency for another.

Looking at myself now I was seeing the same self-hatred that was underneath the surface self-assurance all of the members of my family showed. We were unable to go through life without finding somebody to scapegoat. We had to denigrate others in order to make ourselves feel better and were given to instantaneous judgments and stubborn unwillingness ever to change our minds once we'd made them up.

I'd joked about how I'd never admitted to my brother that I knew the moon is smaller than the earth, an argument we had many years ago, when we were both very young. But the joke was on me because it's not funny to be that stubborn, unforgiving, resentful and unwilling to admit my mistakes.

When I was very young, I was told my mother literally risked her life to bring me into the world. My interpretation of this event was that I was this flawed person. After all, I'd almost killed my mother. I carried such shame and guilt for a long time over that incident. For a long time I felt that I shouldn't have been born.

I remember reading a short story when I was a teenager about a man who was born and died in absolute obscurity. Even official records of his birth and death were destroyed in a fire. It seemed to me that I would like to be that way. Everyone would be better off, I thought, since I was such a disappointment. Clearly this was depressive thinking, but I remember thinking of it as a real answer to the way I felt at the time.

I did a lot of that kind of thinking as I grew up, although I never allowed anyone to know how I felt. The idea of suicide often seemed attractive to me, not because I really wanted to die, but because I wanted things to change for me. I felt that if I were gone, *they* would be sorry that *they* hadn't valued me while I was there.

I still tend to keep my feelings to myself, even when it's appropriate to share them. What does that mean anyway: "appropriate to share my feelings?"

Being shut away from others and feeling this way causes deeply buried resentment. It brings about isolation, occupation with petty things, stifles creativity and wastes one's life in the process of not being fully alive.

What Ellen knows today, because she's in the *process of discovering more* in recovery, is that the only approval she really needs is her own. She's not immune to slipping back into her old people-pleasing habits from time to time. However, she sees the behavior for what it is more quickly now and adjusts her responses accordingly without making harsh judgments of herself.

She knows she needs people in her life and by choosing to let them in, she's changing the context in which she lives her life. Just as she's changed her attitude about herself, she's changed her attitude about others. With her changed attitude has come a great change in her behavior which, in turn, has brought her greater happiness, peace and serenity.

Reaching For Help

Every state has a department devoted to preventing and treating addictions, although not yet for co-dependence, and they have information about short- and long-term treatment centers. It's helpful to have insurance coverage which covers the cost of recovery care, but the federal government has funded programs in every state which defray the cost of treatment. State and federally funded programs are also pledged to anonymity for their clients. Participating in them is a way to protect one's self from the fear of "everyone knowing."

Whether co-dependent women are addicted or not, I always recommend that recovering women seek out an appropriate self-help group. They're the least threatening and the most completely supportive resources available. They are as close as the telephone book and there are members who are glad to accompany newcomers to first meetings.

It's always a good idea not to make up one's mind about the usefulness of this group experience until attending at least six meetings in ACoA or Co-dependents Anonymous groups, or 30 meetings in 30 days for addicts and alcoholics. Responses to the meetings during the beginning will range from total acceptance to great resistance to the experience. It's good to push on past these first responses to see how the experience wears in the long run.

Usually recovering alcoholics or drug addicts who are clean and sober in the beginning of recovery are not psychotic, out of touch with reality or dangerous to themselves or others. Therefore, I never recommend psychiatry or therapy until sobriety has been well established, the danger of relapse is well past and the habit of sobriety has been formed. In my opinion, it's a mistake to push oneself too hard delving into the past and trying to straighten out all the wreckage of the past. In recovery, time is on the side of the person who is honestly trying to come to grips with herself and her life.

After all, the most normal thing in the life of the addict is to reach for a chemical in the middle of emotional turmoil. New strategies for living must be formed with a clear mind, based on an acceptance of her addiction and the changes it will require in her life.

Any good aware therapist would never try to treat someone who comes into his or her office drunk or stoned. As Father John Martin says, it's like "trying to treat someone under anesthesia." It simply cannot be done. However, once sobriety is established, a therapist can augment the work done in self-help groups and vice versa. The work should progress with regard to the recovering person's need to feel safe, keeping her head above water at all times and keeping in mind the very special needs which must be addressed in the context of women's recovery.

Therapy is not marriage. If a woman doesn't feel her therapist is the right one, she should look for another. She should never stay with anyone in a therapeutic relationship if it's not working. She should keep looking until she's found the right person for her.

Hope As An Act Of Self-Love

When I met Mary, she was crippled by muscular dystrophy. She was confined to a wheelchair, but I could picture her before she became unable to stand, moving around energetically, being busy and productive as she went through her day.

Her beautiful spirit was still fully functioning. Physically she was small and delicate, around 34 years old. One of Mary's hobbies was reading "how-to" books because she loved knowing how things worked. She was like that about people, too, and spent time studying them. Like a lot of people with life-threatening illnesses, Mary had little time to spend on people or things that wasted her time.

One night as we sat talking by the fire in her house, Mary told me about the time when she had her first spiritual awakening. She had just graduated from college and was on her way to Europe by boat to spend the summer before starting graduate school.

On the first night out from New York, she went up on deck for a stroll and was thrilled to see the way the sky looked. It was pitch black, except for the stars. As Mary watched, she became overwhelmed with the feeling that she was really so very small and insignificant in relation to the universe. As she stood there humbled by that thought, another pushed its way through, bringing such a sense of joy she could only smile broadly.

She was indeed small and insignificant in relation to the vastness of the universe but she was also the only Mary with exactly that mind and that body, that set of feelings and intuitions the world would ever see. She was unique, irreplaceable and therefore incredibly special.

As she continued to think about it, she began to see that if her life was really special and irreplaceable, then didn't that bring a responsibility to her to make the most of it? It was at that precise point that Mary believed the grace of God entered her life. She made a decision to stop wasting what time was left to her. Later, when the muscular dystrophy was diagnosed, Mary never allowed herself any self-pity. She already knew it was not important how long she lived . . . not that she wanted to die . . . but what she did with the life she had left.

Although Mary seems at first to be an extraordinary person, I've been fortunate to have known a lot of women like her. These are women who, in spite of seemingly overwhelming odds, have pulled their lives out of the fires of pain and hopelessness and have gone on to be wonderful role models for others.

I don't mean they've necessarily done great things which will live after them for centuries. Rather, through the process of sharing their own fears, doubts and insecurities, they have managed to save some of those irreplaceable lives, their own and others.

All of the women I meet in recovery represent Mary to me. They know that in the best of all possible worlds no one has more than the moments at hand to live. Wasting any of it by choice is irrational.

When we were little girls, none of us told our parents that we wanted to grow up to be an addict or a co-dependent, just like them. But having come to grips with the reality that we are one or both of those things, it's our choice to recover.

Even though we may not be able to do it alone, there is plenty of help available for us. It's up to each of us to make the decision that recovery is what we want and the least for which we will settle. When we do that, there is no end to the benefits we may derive from being "a part of the solution, instead of part of the problem."

Suggested Reading

Ackerman, Robert J., **Perfect Daughters.** Deerfield Beach: Health Communications, 1989.

Beattie, Melody, **Co-dependent No More.** San Francisco: Harper/Hazelden, 1987.

Beattie, Melody, **Beyond Co-dependence.** San Francisco: Harper/Hazelden, 1989.

Bolen, Jean Shinoda, **Goddesses In Everywoman.** New York: Harper & Row, 1984.

Cermak, Timmen L., **Co-Dependence.** Minneapolis: Johnson Institute, 1986.

Fishel, Ruth L., **The Journey Within.** Deerfield Beach: Health Communications, 1987.

Fishel, Ruth L., **Learning To Live In The Now.** Deerfield Beach: Health Communications, 1988.

Fishel, Ruth L., **Time For Joy.** Deerfield Beach: Health Communications, 1989.

Jampolsky, Gerald G., **Love Is Letting Go Of Fear.** New York: Bantam Books, 1981.

Levin, Pamela, **Becoming The Way We Are.** Deerfield Beach: Health Communications, 1988.

Miller, Jean Baker, **Toward A New Psychology Of Women.** Boston: Beacon Press, 1976.

Paul, Jordan, and Margaret Paul, **Do I Have To Give Up Me To Be Loved By You?** Minneapolis: CompCare Publications, 1983.

Rich, Adrienne, **On Lies, Secrets And Silence.** New York: W.W. Norton, 1979.

Ryan, Mary P., **Womanhood In America.** New York: Harper & Row, 1975.

Sheehy, Gail, **Passages.** New York: Bantam Books, 1977.

Stuart, Mary S., **In Sickness And In Health.** Deerfield Beach: Health Communications, 1988.

Wegscheider-Cruse, Sharon, and Joseph Cruse, **Understanding Co-dependency.** Deerfield Beach: Health Communications, 1990.

Whitfield, Charles, **Healing The Child Within.** Pompano Beach: Health Communications, 1987.

Whitfield, Charles, **A Gift To Myself.** Deerfield Beach: Health Communications, 1990.

Appendix

Resources

- Al-Anon, Al-Anon
  Adult Children of Alcoholics
  and Alateen Family Groups
  POB 862 Midtown Station
  New York, NY 10018

- Alcoholics Anonymous
  Box 459 Grand Central
  Station
  New York, NY 10163

- Adult Children of Alcoholics
  POB 35623
  Los Angeles, CA 90035

- Batterers Anonymous
  POB 29
  Redlands, CA 92373

- Co-dependents
  Anonymous
  POB 5508
  Glendale, AZ 85312-5508
  (602) 944-0141

- Divorce Anonymous
  POB 5313
  Chicago, IL 60680

- Emotions Anonymous
  POB 4245
  St. Paul, MN 55104

- Families Anonymous
  POB 344
  Torrance, CA 90501

- Families in Action
  Suite 300
  3845 N. Druid Hills Rd.
  Decatur, GA 30033

- Nar-Anon Family Groups
  350 5th St., Suite 207
  San Pedro, CA 90731

- Narcotics Anonymous
  POB 9999
  Van Nuys, CA 91409

- National Single Parent
  Coalition
  10 West 23 Street
  New York, NY 10010

- Overeaters Anonymous
  4025 Spenser St.,
  Suite 203
  Torrance, CA 90503

- Parents Anonymous
  22330 Hawthorne Blvd.
  Torrance, CA 90505

- Parents Without Partners
  7910 Woodmont Ave.
  Washington, DC 20014

- Pill-Anon Family
  Programs
  POB 120 Gracie Station
  New York, NY 10028

- Pills Anonymous
  POB 473 Ansonia
  Station
  New York, NY 10023

- Prison Families
  Anonymous
  134 Jackson Street
  Hempstead, NY 11550

- Single Dad's Hotline
  POB 4842
  Scottsdale, AZ 85258

- Survivors Of Incest
  Anonymous
  P.O. Box 21817
  Baltimore, MD 21222
  (301) 282-3400

New Books . . .
from Health Communications

ALTERNATIVE PATHWAYS TO HEALING: The Recovery Medicine Wheel
Kip Coggins, MSW
This book with its unique approach to recovery explains the concept of the
medicine wheel — and how you can learn to live in harmony with yourself,
with others and with the earth.
ISBN 1-55874-089-9 $7.95

UNDERSTANDING CO-DEPENDENCY
Sharon Wegscheider-Cruse, M.A., and Joseph R. Cruse, M.D.
The authors give us a basic understanding of co-dependency that everyone
can use — what it is, how it happens, who is affected by it and what can
be done for them.
ISBN 1-55874-077-5 $7.95

THE OTHER SIDE OF THE FAMILY:
A Book For Recovery From Abuse, Incest And Neglect
Ellen Ratner, Ed.M.
This workbook addresses the issues of the survivor — self-esteem, feelings,
defenses, grieving, relationships and sexuality — and goes beyond to help
them through the healing process.
ISBN 1-55874-110-0 $13.95

OVERCOMING PERFECTIONISM:
The Key To A Balanced Recovery
Ann W. Smith, M.S.
This book offers practical hints, together with a few lighthearted ones, as a
guide toward learning to "live in the middle." It invites you to let go of your
superhuman syndrome and find a balanced recovery.
ISBN 1-55874-111-9 $8.95

LEARNING TO SAY NO:
Establishing Healthy Boundaries
Carla Wills-Brandon, M.A.
If you grew up in a dysfunctional family, establishing boundaries is a
difficult and risky decision. Where do you draw the line? Learn to recognize
yourself as an individual who has the power to say no.
ISBN 1-55874-087-2 $8.95

3201 S.W. 15th Street,
Deerfield Beach, FL 33442-8190
1-800-851-9100

**Health
Communications, Inc.**

Daily Affirmation Books from . . .
Health Communications

GENTLE REMINDERS FOR CO-DEPENDENTS: Daily Affirmations
Mitzi Chandler

With insight and humor, Mitzi Chandler takes the co-dependent and the adult child through the year. Gentle Reminders is for those in recovery who seek to enjoy the miracle each day brings.

ISBN 1-55874-020-1   **$6.95**

TIME FOR JOY: Daily Affirmations
Ruth Fishel

With quotations, thoughts and healing energizing affirmations these daily messages address the fears and imperfections of being human, guiding us through self-acceptance to a tangible peace and the place within where there is *time for joy.*

ISBN 0-932194-82-6   **$6.95**

AFFIRMATIONS FOR THE INNER CHILD
Rokelle Lerner

This book contains powerful messages and helpful suggestions aimed at adults who have unfinished childhood issues. By reading it daily we can end the cycle of suffering and move from pain into recovery.

ISBN 1-55874-045-6   **$6.95**

DAILY AFFIRMATIONS: For Adult Children of Alcoholics
Rokelle Lerner

Affirmations are a way to discover personal awareness, growth and spiritual potential, and self-regard. Reading this book gives us an opportunity to nurture ourselves, learn who we are and what we want to become.

ISBN 0-932194-47-3
(Little Red Book)   **$6.95**
(New Cover Edition)   **$6.95**

SOOTHING MOMENTS: Daily Meditations For Fast-Track Living
Bryan E. Robinson, Ph.D.

This is designed for those leading fast-paced and high-pressured lives who need time out each day to bring self-renewal, joy and serenity into their lives.

ISBN 1-55874-075-9   **$6.95**

3201 S.W. 15th Street,
Deerfield Beach, FL 33442-8190
1-800-851-9100

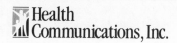

Health Communications, Inc.

Helpful 12-Step Books from . . .
Health Communications

12 STEPS TO SELF-PARENTING For Adult Children
Philip Oliver-Diaz, M.S.W., and Patricia A. O'Gorman, Ph.D.

This gentle 12-Step guide takes the reader from pain to healing and self-parenting, from anger to forgiveness, and from fear and despair to recovery.

ISBN 0-932194-68-0   **$7.95**

SELF-PARENTING 12-STEP WORKBOOK: Windows To Your Inner Child
Patricia O'Gorman, Ph.D., and Philip Oliver-Diaz, M.S.W.

This workbook invites you to become the complete individual you were born to be by using visualizations, exercises and experiences designed to reconnect you to your inner child.

ISBN 1-55874-052-X   **$9.95**

THE 12-STEP STORY BOOKLETS
Mary M. McKee

Each beautifully illustrated booklet deals with a step, using a story from nature in parable form. The 12 booklets (one for each step) lead us to a better understanding of ourselves and our recovery.

ISBN 1-55874-002-3   **$8.95**

VIOLENT VOICES:
12 Steps To Freedom From Emotional And Verbal Abuse
Kay Porterfield, M.A.

By using the healing model of the 12 Steps emotionally abused women are shown how to deal effectively with verbal and psychological abuse and to begin living as healed and whole people.

ISBN 1-55874-028-7   **$9.95**

GIFTS FOR PERSONAL GROWTH & RECOVERY
Wayne Kritsberg

A goldmine of positive techniques for recovery (affirmations, journal writing, visualizations, guided meditations, etc.), this book is indispensable for those seeking personal growth.

ISBN 0-932194-60-5   **$6.95**

3201 S.W. 15th Street,
Deerfield Beach, FL 33442-8190
1-800-851-9100

Health Communications, Inc.

Other Books By . . .
Health Communications

ADULT CHILDREN OF ALCOHOLICS
Janet Woititz

Over a year on *The New York Times* Best-Seller list, this book is the primer on Adult Children of Alcoholics.

ISBN 0-932194-15-X   **$6.95**

STRUGGLE FOR INTIMACY
Janet Woititz

Another best-seller, this book gives insightful advice on learning to love more fully.

ISBN 0-932194-25-7   **$6.95**

BRADSHAW ON: THE FAMILY: A Revolutionary Way of Self-Discovery
John Bradshaw

The host of the nationally televised series of the same name shows us how families can be healed and individuals can realize full potential.

ISBN 0-932194-54-0   **$9.95**

HEALING THE SHAME THAT BINDS YOU
John Bradshaw

This important book shows how toxic shame is the core problem in our compulsions and offers new techniques of recovery vital to all of us.

ISBN 0-932194-86-9   **$9.95**

HEALING THE CHILD WITHIN: Discovery and Recovery for
Adult Children of Dysfunctional Families — Charles Whitfield, M.D.

Dr. Whitfield defines, describes and discovers how we can reach our Child Within to heal and nurture our woundedness.

ISBN 0-932194-40-0   **$8.95**

A GIFT TO MYSELF: A Personal Guide To Healing My Child Within
Charles L. Whitfield, M.D.

Dr. Whitfield provides practical guidelines and methods to work through the pain and confusion of being an Adult Child of a dysfunctional family.

ISBN 1-55874-042-2   **$11.95**

HEALING TOGETHER: A Guide To Intimacy And Recovery For
Co-dependent Couples — Wayne Kritsberg, M.A.

This is a practical book that tells the reader why he or she gets into dysfunctional and painful relationships, and then gives a concrete course of action on how to move the relationship toward health.

ISBN 1-55784-053-8   **$8.95**

3201 S.W. 15th Street,
Deerfield Beach, FL 33442-8190
1-800-851-9100

Health Communications, Inc.